GRADES DON'T MATTER

Using Assessment To Measure True Learning

GRADES DON'T MATTER

Using Assessment To Measure True Learning

TONY DONEN

with Jennifer Anton, Lisa Beard,
Todd Stinson, and Glenda Sullivan

Grades Don't Matter: Using Assessment to Measure True Learning

ISBN: 978-1-936541-07-2
Published by Armour&Armour Publications

10 9 8 7 6 5 4 3 2

Contents

INTRODUCTION

Tony Donen
Principal

I'M NOT SURE which day it was or what grade I was examining, but I do remember the epiphany: The grades I was examining didn't make much sense.

How could little Joey have a 95 in AP Calculus and score a 1 on the AP exam? How could Susie have a 69 and receive a grade of F when she clearly knew pretty much all of the material in the class? Why did we continue to spend our time debating what percentage to assign to tests, quizzes, and homework for courses in a given department? What exactly was the magic percentage?

I kept asking myself these questions and many more when talking to kids, parents, and teachers about grades. Heck, I spent more time talking about grades than probably any other item

I can recall—and no matter the situation, I was constantly convincing myself that a good grade meant the student was learning and performing at a high level and that a bad grade meant the student clearly didn't know what was happening in the class.

Unfortunately, it took me more than three years to figure out that the grade didn't reflect anything I thought it had. That could have happened much sooner if I had paid attention to a first-year teacher in her fourth week of teaching. But I'll explain that soon enough.

In my second year as principal, I was so proud of our school. Achievement scores had come up on our standardized state tests, and our kids were doing really well. At least it appeared that way. In my first year I had noticed that the students didn't take the state tests very seriously and had little motivation to do so. So I decided that I would get the kids excited and motivated through some incentives.

First, I took all ten of the "important" state and national tests and showed the average score for our school from the prior year to the senior class. I told them for every test our school showed improvement, they would earn a half day of senior time at the end of the year.

The seniors loved it. And the results were dramatic. We showed improvement in every test. I gave the seniors a full week of "senior time," and everyone was happy. Central Office staff were happy, students were proud, teachers were proud, and I was excited about how much our students had apparently learned.

I was so proud that I told the tenth graders the next year that for every 0.1 on the PLAN they improved, I would run around the track one time. The PLAN assessment is the tenth-grade version of the ACT, similar to what the PSAT is to the SAT. Significant gain for groups on the PLAN would be improvement by 0.9 points or more, and since I didn't expect significant gain, I felt relatively safe on how far I would possibly have to run. Again, though, the kids gave a more complete effort than in the past, and the tenth grade scores went up 2.0 points from the previous year. I had to run twenty laps (five miles) around the track with the entire school watching. Ouch! But once again, I was impressed with our apparent student learning.

It wasn't until my third year that I began to notice that there was an underlying culture of what I like to refer to as "grade compliance."

We began the year by explaining to students that if they had a failing grade, they would have to stay after school for an additional period until all their grades were passing. Then all of the apparent achievement I thought was taking place began to unravel in my mind. On our first day we mandated students to stay after school, approximately thirty-five percent of the student body had to stay. It quickly dropped to about twenty to twenty-five percent, but the decrease was not because the students had learned more. The reason for more passing grades was simply that students became more compliant and completed more assignments.

About two weeks into doing our mandatory after-school period, which we called ninth period (we had an eight-period day), a first-year teacher walked up to me after the period and said: "Ninth period doesn't have anything to do with learning. They are completing the work, but they are not learning." Of course, I heard what she said, but I didn't really *listen* to what she had said. It took me two more years to truly understand the power in her statement.

In my first four years as principal, I had created a school that could do very well on minimum proficiency state testing. Yet even with those scores higher than at any other time in our school's history, something just didn't seem "right" about our assessment practices. Our completion and compliance were good enough to meet minimum standards, but we could see no proof of learning at more than a minimal level.

At the end of the second year of ninth period, I was exhausted and increasingly frustrated. I began looking very closely at student grades down to every individual assignment, and this is what I found:

Grades were a culmination of random percentage weights

on different types of assignments with little forethought into what the grades were telling us about the learning that we were supposed to be holding in the highest esteem.

Many grades were based on the luck of which teacher a student had for class. In all classes, many grades were based on such work habits as doing work on time and complying with teacher requests as opposed to verifying that learning did take place for a specific target.

Grades continued to be an individual teacher's sole possession, and student success was based primarily on completing work. No student or parent could explain what a grade of 60 really meant in terms of learning as opposed to an 85. Teachers felt they could explain it, but more often than not the explanation from a teacher's point of view still came back to what a student needed to *complete*. An explanation of mastery of material was usually secondary, and mastery of a particular learning target was almost never explained. The problem in this system is that the student does not claim any ownership over his or her learning, and the teacher is the only one in the process who can—and therein lies the underlying problem with this approach to grading.

To emphasize this point further: We assumed that the best explanation for comparing students was that the kid with an 85 was better than the kid with the 60, but we couldn't give specific reasons why. Well, I take that back. We probably would have said something like, "Jimmy turns his work in on time. If Jane had, her grade would be better." We might have said something else that had nothing to do with what the students actually knew or didn't know. Eighty-five is just better than 60. It just is.

To me it came down to two basic items: completion versus mastery. And it was clear that every grade we assigned could speak to completion and very few could tell me something about student mastery. Students were playing school, and everyone was happy.

In every school in every location in every system, grades are the real test of what a school deems important. You can throw out everything else when figuring out what your school is about. Take a couple of gradebooks and look at how you grade the students. That will tell you what your school values.

There is no perfect gradebook or assessment process. But there are certainly better grading practices, and our role as educators is to promote student learning as our top priority. *This should not be optional, ignored, or confused with compliant behaviors.* Grades are meant to inform students on what they do well, what they need to strengthen, and what steps can be taken to increase the learning. And they should not be secretive or a surprise; they should be transparent and something that an individual student can explain in depth as they relate to his own learning.

And so it was that, in the spring of my fourth year, I invited ten teachers to throw out their traditional gradebooks and start over. We would begin to create a school culture that was all about learning. I picked teachers ranging from those in their first years of teaching to savvy veterans, and from high achievers to the ones who will try anything. I separated the ten into two groups of five and had each group meet with a lead teacher to facilitate the conversation. The lead teacher met with both groups.

The sole requirement I gave the group was to create a gradebook system based on student mastery of content. At that time, I didn't have any more real knowledge of what to do and couldn't find any particular examples of where this even happened. They had one basic goal: to have the gradebook reflect student mastery of concepts. Their gradebooks needed to show that and simply that.

The result of their work was to focus on four levels of mastery for students: Non-Mastery, Initial Mastery, Mastery, and Advanced Mastery. They proceeded to use NM, IM, M, and AM for many of the grades they placed in their gradebooks. Predictably, a major focus of the conversation was what numerical grade these categories would become. After much debate, they agreed to a system of NM = 0, IM = 70, M = 85, and AM = 100, with 70 as the minimum passing grade. The other practice they initiated in their gradebooks was to break student assignments into overriding categories that we called essential outcomes (which varied from teacher to teacher). Each assignment fell under one of the essential outcomes and received a mastery rating that reflects level of learning. The result was a gradebook in which, for the most part, students had an overriding grade for each essential outcome.

As with any new endeavor, the results were all over the place. Some teachers and classes absolutely shined. Then there were teachers who thought this was insane and that I had lost my mind.

Teachers and students had conversations that were based on what students needed to learn and what the student knew and at what level. And for the first time in my years in education, I actually could see a distinct difference in the student–teacher relationship, specifically the relationship that resulted in assigning student grades.

I don't think I can tell you how many times I have gone through discipline conferences with students and ended up saying something to the effect of "actions speak louder than words." It's time for us as educators to apply that to our methods. Every single action we as educators take prior to assigning grades defines the learning we expect to occur in our schools. Until we evaluate and understand each action we take and we are clear and intentional with each step, we will be as desperate as the student who continues to show up in the principal's office.

The purpose of this book is three-fold. The first is the most obvious. We hope that our first efforts will lead others into the grading process and create a learning culture through a grading process that actually values learning. We believe that our ideas, challenges, roadblocks, and successes can help others find practical ways to make this process successful in real-world settings.

The second purpose is for our school and teachers. We wanted a way for our staff not only to work toward completing this endeavor but also to have an outlet to showcase and write about their journey. It is a way for us to record this experience and make ourselves accountable for moving forward in our own process.

And the last purpose is purely personal. I have two little girls. By "little" I also mean very young, energetic, optimistic, and eager to learn. They have no idea what it means to be given a grade, but they will. My hope is that when they do, it will be a reflection of learning and not a reflection of compliance or completion. I hope they will be able to explain what learning targets they know, what they can apply, and where they are not showing understanding. In other words, I hope they will have the opportunity to go to a school where the grade is a reflection of learning.

This book is a compilation of our thoughts, ideas, and vision to create a true learning culture in a traditional high school setting. More than that, it introduces you to the high school teachers who made their own transformations by changing assessment practices. We hope you will find the book an interesting account as well as an impetus to change the practices taking place in your classroom and school, and to define what you value.

I wish you the best as you dive into this book. Not everything we have done or are doing is the best, though that is our desire. We hope you enjoy our account and that it provides you with an urgency to answer the questions: What do you value in your classroom, and what does your gradebook reflect?

1

The Ten

Tony Donen
Principal

I WAS SITTING at a conference titled "Failure is Not an Option" in the fall semester of the 2006–2007 school year. Each speaker at the conference talked about how to impact kids, and the speakers were entertaining, compelling, and invigorating. Everyone in the audience (approximately four hundred of us) was smiling, nodding, and soaking it in.

If you have ever been to a conference with charismatic and engaging speakers, you can probably relate to this experience and how it invigorated you. The messages sent to our heads first touched our hearts. But seldom do those messages ever come close to answering "that question." You know the question—the question every teacher asks: What specifically can I do to make the gains needed in my classroom?

The speakers who captured our hearts and minds aimed at answering this question. They told stories and made us laugh and even cry as they talked about the core principles of relationships, relevance, and engagement. However, these insights do not come with a formula; you can't just tell someone to do steps 1, 2, and 3, and the success will happen. Instead, it's about building relationships with the students, finding relevance in your curriculum, and designing lessons that engage students. Accomplishing this relies on your creativity and personal experiences, shaped by your own personality and your natural disposition.

There is no "right" answer or straightforward steps to answering "that question." It is a combination of many different variables. Anyone who tells you there is one distinct way to have great relationships with every one of your students or to catch their unbridled attention is simply not telling you the truth. It hasn't been found because we all are different. But as the four hundred of us sat in that conference hall, we believed in the power of the relationship, the strength of the relevance of our instruction, and the commitment to engaging our students. And we should. However, these are attributes always to pursue, not structured and outlined steps that can be handed to you.

So why was this conference so important to my enlightenment to learning? It happened with perhaps the driest and least-compelling presenter.

At the end of one of the conference days, as a presenter went up to the podium we expected a presentation similar to those before, which featured a high entertainment value. Yet her presentation was in sharp contrast to the others. And her message was the most important. Changing student achievement can be done in many different ways, she said, but take some time to study the research. What we would find is that ultimately the Number One, top of the list, most crucial piece in making achievement gains for any teacher is . . . assessment practices. It is not even close.

She offered us two options: You can rely on trying to create a perfect lesson for every student, every day, challenged by the millions of variables ever-present, or you can tackle the most difficult and most influential piece of the teaching process, assessment.

When she was finished, most people preferred what the other speakers had to say. Why? None of us became teachers because our heads said logically this is what we are meant to do with our lives. We all became teachers because of our hearts. It is the emotion of teaching that drives us to teach. But it is not the emotion of teaching that has the most impact on learning. It is our assessment practices that most dictate student achievement. And so, when this presenter left the podium, she didn't receive a standing ovation like many of the other speakers. Who wants to work on assessment when we can spend time on items more compelling to our hearts?

Ironically, this question does have an easy answer. Who wants to work on assessment instead of more compelling topics? It's the educators who are tired of mediocrity and want to help all students achieve at high levels, not just the kids who make us feel good because they want to be with us. It's about helping each kid achieve at high levels.

At this point I was sick of trying to work on everything. I was ready to put aside my personal likes and my own pet ideas, and to focus instead on what research said, giving attention to an area that is easy to ignore. Assessment is the key . . . no matter how glittering the other aspects of teaching appear to be, or your own personal desires for that matter. When you decide that you want to maximize your effect in the classroom, you also will have to make a conscious effort to become an expert in your assessment practices.

And so, after a few more months of wanting to ignore assessment, I finally sat down with one of my math teachers, and we began our quest to use assessment to measure learning. With the very little knowledge I had on exactly how to do that and the limited amount of information I could find on this actually happening in a high school setting, we decided to begin with the most obvious and blatant area of assessment: the gradebook. With the help of Todd Stinson, a math teacher at the time and later our assistant principal, I selected ten teachers to work with Todd to build a gradebook based on mastery of teaching outcomes, and we built the gradebook ideas from scratch. Oh, and just to increase the challenge, I also wanted each of these teachers to implement it in our fourth nine-week term in at least one of their classes. In other words, I expected nothing short of a miracle.

The original group of ten teachers was:

- Todd Stinson
- George Mast, computer teacher
- Tiffany Johnson, English teacher
- Rudy Gilchrist, Spanish teacher
- Valerie Willmore, science teacher
- Lisa Beard, science teacher
- Andy Fleenor, math teacher
- Carol Moth, art teacher
- Kate Burgun, English teacher
- Chris Whitefield, history teacher.

In this book, you will find excerpts from all of them except for Carol, Kate, and Chris. Carol retired, Kate moved to another school district, and Chris moved to another school before we began writing the book. Along with insights from the original group, you also will find a variety of experiences from others who followed the first group to provide multiple perspectives on the changes that began to take place in their classrooms and our school.

To start at the beginning, Todd Stinson sets the stage for our culture of change.

■

Todd Stinson
Former Math Teacher and Current Assistant Principal

I CAN REMEMBER having two thoughts immediately after Mr. Donen presented me with the idea of leading a team focusing on changing the way that we assessed students. The first thought was that it made sense. For nearly eight years I had struggled with students' grades. At the end of each school year, I thought of students who either "passed" my class but were able to complete little of the material or students who "failed" my class who I *knew* could solve any type of problem that I placed in front of them. Assessment based on the mastery of standards and skills solved this problem.

My second thought was that I had no idea how to begin. Not only was Mr. Donen asking (or telling) me to change my own classroom practices, but he also expected me to help others with their transition. I thought he was out of his mind. But he was my boss, so I agreed to "lead" the team.

Mr. Donen and I hand-picked the team. It consisted of teachers from a variety of content areas and experience levels, from a second-year English teacher to a veteran art teacher, some we thought who would be very open to the idea and those that we knew would be less receptive. The only common strand was that we felt that they truly wanted to give students better and more accurate gauges of what they could and could not do in terms of academic content.

We met one day in the early spring with the expectation of creating a framework for implementing our new system during the last quarter of the school year. Our discussion ranged from "What exactly are we trying to accomplish?" to "How will this affect GPA?" to "Why me?" Through much deliberation we developed a four-tiered system of grading:

- NM for Non-Mastery
- IM for Initial Mastery
- M for Mastery
- AM for Advanced Mastery.

We struggled with the notion that each of us could and, in fact, had to decide what each of these labels looked like in our individual classrooms. However, with varying degrees of enthusiasm, we all left the conference room that day committing to implement this plan in at least one of our classes in the upcoming grading period.

Looking back, the day did not go as I had expected it to. I knew it would be difficult to get ten teachers to buy into this notion. But I did not expect the difficulty to lie in the area where it did. The majority of the first day was not spent on debating the merits of this type of assessment, but rather on how we were going to convert this feedback to numeric scores. It was tough to contemplate throwing out the only grading system that most of us had known our entire lives, from kindergarten to the present.

I chose to try this out on my Advanced Algebra and Trigonometry class, a class of about twenty-five seniors, most of whom had been in my Algebra II class the previous year. I went in on the Monday following our Assessment Team meeting armed with a plan that I laid out to the kids. From this point on, they would have three chances to prove to me that they could master a skill and successfully solve problems based on the standards I had chosen as important. (These were labeled "essential outcomes" by Mr. Donen.)

The first opportunity was on homework, the second on a quiz, the third on a test. Although it did not drastically change how I taught, it did alter the number and type of problems I assigned as homework. I felt that since I intended to use homework as a factor in their overall grade, I needed to grade every problem that I assigned. This cut the number of homework problems by about two-thirds. Also, I was very careful that each of the problems I assigned offered an opportunity to practice the skills intended. After returning the graded homework to the students, we discussed the problems and set a date for the quiz. In general, a quiz would cover two essential outcomes.

An example quiz for one essential outcome (which I called EO3: Using the Law of Cosines) is in Figure 1-1. I would grade the quizzes, return them, and move forward with the material. Figure 1-2 is the rubric I would use to score the quiz. This, like most of my rubrics, was a basic tool that assigned a level of mastery to the student assessment that was determined by the percentage of problems that the student completed correctly.

FIG. 1-1: "Law of Cosines" quiz

Algebra / Trig. Name____________
Quiz EO3 Date____________
Fourth Nine Weeks

Use the Law of Cosines to find the missing sides and angles of the following triangles.

1. A = 38°, b = 5, c = 12: find a
2. C = 82°, a = 11, b = 14: find c
3. a = 2, b = 5, C = 60°: find c
4. a = 10, c = 8, B = 45°: find b, A, and C
5. Find the distance across the lake from A to C, to the nearest foot, using the measurements shown in the figure.

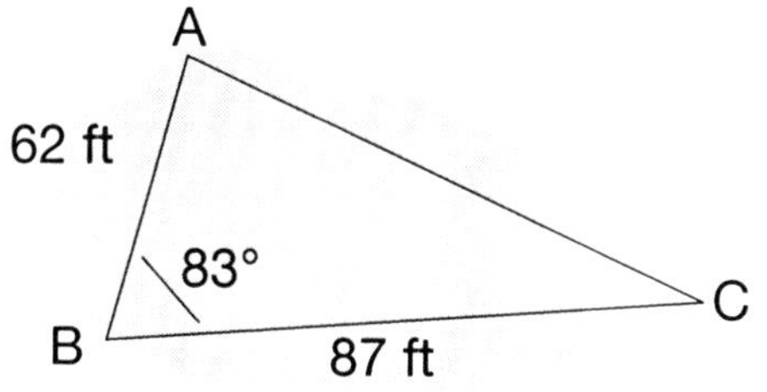

FIG. 1-2: Rubric for grading "Law of Cosines" quiz

Number Correct	Mastery Level
0	Not Mastered
1	Not Mastered
2	Not Mastered
3	Initially Mastered
4	Mastered
5	Advanced Mastery

Since students would have three opportunities (graded homework, quiz, and test) where they were assessed on each essential outcome, my responsibility was to determine an overall level of mastery for that essential outcome. This was the only part on which I was a little fuzzy. I looked at a variety of factors: Did the student show steady progress on the topic? Did the student start off strong, only to fade on the test? Did the student choose not to do the homework at all, and take a chance on the quiz and test? Figure 1-3 denotes several different combinations of the three scores and what I used for the final essential outcome grade.

FIG. 1-3: Overall grades for "Law of Cosines"

	Homework	Quiz	Test	Overall Grade
Student A	M	M	M	Mastery
Student B	NM	IM	M	Mastery
Student C	Missing	AM	AM	Advanced Mastery
Student D	AM	M	IM	Mastery
Student E	IM	IM	NM	Non-Mastery

The other piece that left me with a sense of discomfort was the notion of allowing students to retake tests, but I put it in place anyway. If students were unhappy with their grades on a skill, they could redo any of the three assessments until they reached Advanced Mastery. Figure 1-4 is an example of an assessment for redoing the Law of Cosines quiz.

FIG. 1-4: "Law of Cosines" requiz

Algebra / Trig. Name____________
Quiz EO3 (Requiz) Date____________
Fourth Nine Weeks

Use the Law of Cosines to find the missing sides and angles of the following triangles.

1. A = 24°, b = 4, c = 11: find a
2. C = 78°, a = 8, b = 17: find c
3. a = 4, b = 10, C = 65°: find c
4. a = 11, c = 7, B = 42°: find b, A, and C
5. Find the distance from Campsite A to Campsite B, to the nearest kilometer, using the measurements shown in the figure.

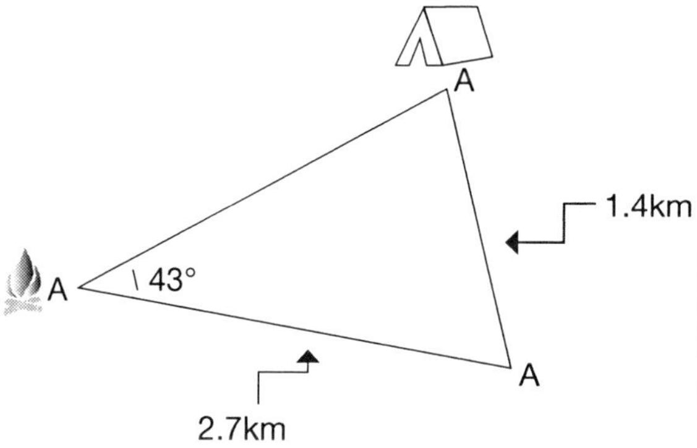

The students hated it. And they were not afraid to let me know it. The biggest complaint I heard during the first week of my implementation was that their papers no longer had a grade on them, only one of the levels of mastery. The students felt like I was trying to pull something over on them. They didn't trust that this was going to benefit them in the long run, no matter how many times I assured them that it would. I heard over and over, "What's my grade?" And I explained again and again that it was about understanding the material and being able to apply the material to solve problems. Still, they wanted a numeric grade.

■

Rudy Gilchrist
Spanish Teacher

GRADES! GRADES! What's my grade? Why does my son have X grade in your class?

The need for clarity on the issue of grades has long been important. The driving force has been one of justification. I have experienced great pressure as a teacher in being able to demonstrate a clear mathematical relationship between my content and the grades given to my students. As a foreign language teacher, I found that many adults disavow any understanding of my subject and yet want a clear meaning of the grades in my class. So I had long ago turned to my version of "mastery."

The practice work done during class didn't really matter. Pronunciation, conversation, and cultural learning were too open to apparent subjectivity for clear assessments. So I focused on vocabulary and grammar. The tests based on vocabulary and grammar had right or wrong answers, and the students' grades related directly to the number correct. No one could debate the clear mastery nor the veracity of the grades . . . except me. This grading practice kept us from moving beyond a very rudimentary class.

I smiled when Mr. Donen introduced the idea of mastery learning. I had been given carte blanche to revamp my grading practices. Armed with the mastery scale (NM, IM, M, AM) and rubrics, I could clarify and quantify any type of lesson. I could also manage the time-consuming process of grading complex work through the format provided by the use of rubrics.

One example of this is a pronunciation assessment. To assess the students' pronunciation skills I created a rubric that was not dependent on the text but rather on their abilities. An example of the pronunciation assessment follows. Figure 1-5 is a sample text the students read. Figure 1-6 is the instrument used to grade their efforts, and Figure 1-7 is a sample student's results.

Text-specific assessments were arduous because all possible "wrong answers" had to be counted to calculate the percentage of the total. The rubric approach clarified and quantified what each level of mastery would be and thereby streamlined the assessment process. The mastery approach allowed the focus of learning to move from content to students' skill levels.

FIG. 1-5: Sample text

Te Presento a un Amigo
Diólogo

Marta: Hola, María. ¿Qué tal las vacaciones?
María: Hola, Marta. Pues, muy bien, ¿y tú?
Marta: Excelente. Oye, ¿quién es aquel chico guapo cerca de la cafetería?
María: ¿El chico moreno, con la camiseta azul? Es Roberto, un buen amigo mío.
Marta: ¿Puedes presentármelo? Parece muy simpático e inteligente.
María: ¡Por supuesto! Roberto, quiero presentarte a mi amiga, Marta Martínez. Marta, te presento a Roberto González.
Marta: Mucho gusto de conocerte.
Roberto: Igualmente. El gusto es mío. Marta Martínez . . . mmmm. . . ¿Es tu madre profesora de música en el Instituto?
Marta: Sí, exactamente. ¿Por qué?
Roberto: Ella es mi profesora de guitarra clásica. Me encanta su clase. Oye, ¿quieres ir conmigo al concierto el viernes que viene?
Marta: ¡Fantástico! Me gustaría mucho.
María: ¡Pero, Marta, tenemos planes para el cine!
Marta: Lo siento, María, pero no puedo resistir la invitación.

FIG. 1-6: Rubric

Rubric	Advanced Mastery	Mastery	Initial Mastery	Non-Mastery
Pronunciation	0 mistakes	1 mistake	2 mistakes	3+ mistakes
Intonation	0 mistakes	1 mistake	2 mistakes	3+ mistakes
Memorization	0 mistakes	1 mistake	2 mistakes	3+ mistakes

FIG. 1-7: Sample results

Name: Fred Silvers	Date: 3/3/09		Source: Te Presento a un Amigo	
Pronunciation	__0__	_____	_____	_____
Intonation	__0__	__1__	__2__	_____
Memorization	__0__	__1__	__2__	__3__

Fred did a great job with his pronunciation. He said the words perfectly. However, his intonation was off. He had difficulty with the memorization, which gave him problems saying the words with the correct emotive qualities.

The classroom implementation of mastery learning went fairly smoothly for me. My students were already used to the idea that what they learned was what counted (in so far as what was tested). The rubrics we began to use gave them a clear idea of what they needed to be able to do and how the assessment would take place. The classroom began to be more interesting in that a wider variety of activities could viably take place.

The students were shown how each type of grade would be viewed as a progressive analysis of their skill levels. This type of categorization gave a much better picture of the student in terms of strengths and weaknesses. I could then more precisely aim my classroom attention to individual students during different types of lessons/practice. The feedback provided by mastery learning fostered conversations about students and their abilities, rather than the classic generalization, "You need to get your work done and make sure you study tonight."

Mastery learning opened many doors and answered many questions for me. The mastery scale takes the focus away from "grades" and shifts it to assessment. Rubrics allow for clear expectations, assessments, and feedback for student and teacher dialogues. Content becomes embedded in student skill and is evidenced in what the students can do instead of what they "know."

The process is evolutionary. Still, as each teacher tailors the process there is some potential for students to be confused between the various directions that teachers take. I have had to talk through some conflict with "That's not how Mrs. Y said things work!" I think that the potential for quality improvement in my classes clearly outweighs any immediate conflict and that continuing to develop the mastery learning approach is well worth the effort.

■

Tiffany Johnson
English Teacher

I HAD BEEN teaching in my own classroom for only two years when I was presented with a new way of looking at assessment. It might seem odd for someone who had only been teaching for two years at the time to be so averse to change. Assessment? You mean like tests? Mastery what? Mastery learning!? Oh great, the next "new" innovation in education. How long will it last this time, and can't you see that this just doesn't work for English?

I will be the first to admit, I didn't have the best attitude about changing our assessment practices at Fairview High. My AP English IV students also were not pleased with this "new-age grading"; after all, they were accustomed to the old system and were certain that they were going to a college that also used the old system.

The mastery learning grading scale still makes me shudder a bit. There were letters AM (Advanced Mastery = 100), M (Mastery = 85), IM (Initial Mastery = 70) and NM (Non-Mastery = 0). Yet, to me, it didn't feel fair to give a 100 when a test wasn't perfect, but an 85 is much too low for missing one answer. On the flip side, a zero is much too low where a 70 is often too high.

To say the least, I did not agree with that scale at all. Many of us grumbled that this was just a way to make all students pass. Plus, many teachers remembered "Mastery Learning" from the 1980s and were not happy to be hearing about it again.

However, as we began actually discussing assessment, I came to realize many things. First, although it still mattered greatly to the students, the numbers weren't as important as the meaning behind the letters. For example, a student should be able to look at a paper graded IM and realize, "I need to work on this skill," instead of, "Well, at least I'm passing with a 70." However, that is a tough concept to get students to realize. Many students are very grade-driven, while others really don't seem to care at all. Some students will always strive for a higher grade, and still others are content with any grade A through F.

But I gave it a try. I hated it. As I mentioned before, the students also weren't big fans. I still hate those letters and the numbers they represented. But you know what? It made me think. It sometimes is quite hard to have a 1 to 100 scale for grading. For example, for an essay, what is the subtle difference that awards one student a 98, but gives another student a 96? Sometimes rubrics clearly delineate the difference between a 98 and a 96, but then teachers run the very real risk of inflated grades—especially when we have to add an additional three or five points for an honors or AP class. Also, sometimes, although I understand and can explain the reason one student got a 98 versus a 96, often the student, to whom this information is *most* important, cannot decipher it.

I struggled with the changes. I hated having to explain what the letters meant every day. I was frustrated with the lack of flexibility. Needless to say, I was hoping this would just go away, but it didn't. At the end of the year, I was told that I had to do it in at least one class the next year.

■

Lisa Beard
Science Teacher

THE BEST WORD to describe my initial reaction to implementing mastery learning in the classroom is fear. I felt as if everything that I have done in the past—my course syllabus, my grading policies, my course assignments—were about to get a major overhaul and leave me feeling like a first-year teacher all over again.

Once the fears subsided, then the pride stepped in reminding me that I earned this rite of passage; after all, I have been teaching for more than a decade and I, Great Chemistry Teacher, being all-knowing, know best how to be the assessor of my students.

I reasoned that students needed lots of grades in the record book to show that they were actively learning the objectives. I reasoned that applying penalties to grades for behaviors such as late work and poor participation was a necessity in teaching responsible behavior. I reasoned that the only way to be "fair" about a student's GPA was to allow only one opportunity for a student to test. Thus, if the student succeeded, great! And, if he or she failed, better luck on the next objective.

It took a humbling act of self-assessment to conclude that my biggest fear was grading students on what they really know.

I was one of the original ten people chosen to pilot the mastery learning initiative in our high school. During the last quarter of our school year, we each agreed to choose a minimum of one class to assess solely on mastery of the learning objectives.

My original grading scale only had four numeric grades:

- Advanced Mastery (AM) = 100
- Mastery (M) = 85
- Initial Mastery (IM) = 70
- Non-Mastery (NM) = 0.

This grading scale included homework, lab reports, and tests. During the first four weeks, student response was overwhelmingly negative. Students who normally pass by the skin of their teeth were now failing miserably. Students who normally made A's were mad that students who had been making 70s and 80s were now passing with 100s due to retesting.

I was working myself to the bone, making out new assessments for students, coming up with new assignments for those who did not master the original assignments (or failed to turn them in), finding time for tutoring individual students outside of class, calling parents of the miserably failing students, and making time to administer retests. (An example of a part of a test can be found in Figure 1-8, and an example of a part of one retest that I would make is in Figure 1-9.)

It wasn't until the second half of the quarter that I realized that we were on the right track when a student told me that he did not like this "mastery thing" because it meant "I have to know what I am doing." By the end of the quarter, students had a new perspective about the content I was teaching. Their behavior had become intrinsic in nature and focused on the learning essentials of the course.

FIG. 1-8: Test

Naming and Writing Formulas for Ionic Compounds
You may not use your polyatomic ion chart for Part I.
I. Name the following ionic compounds.

1. $NaBr$
2. $Al(OH)_3$
3. NH_4I
4. Li_2SO_4
5. $Cu(NO_2)_2$

II. Write the formulas for the following ionic compounds.

6. sodium acetate
7. iron (II) phosphate
8. lead (IV) hydroxide
9. copper (II) chlorate
10. magnesium phosphate

FIG. 1-9: Re-test A

Naming and Writing Formulas for Ionic Compounds
You may not use your polyatomic ion chart for Part I.
I. Name the following ionic compounds.

1. $AgNO_3$
2. $KMnO_4$
3. Pb_3N
4. $NaCl$
5. K_2SO_4

II. Write the formulas for the following ionic compounds.

6. ammonium oxide
7. cobalt (II) carbonate
8. potassium hydroxide
9. calcium nitrate
10. lead (IV) phosphate

The school year ended on a high note for me when one of my struggling students came up to me after handing in his final exam and asked me to show him once again how to work a stoichiometry problem that was on the exam. This act was evidence to me that the student valued the learning objective more than the numeric grade.

■

Tony Donen
Principal

ULTIMATELY, I WAS not sure that the group's decision to use specific scores and a NM, IM, M, and AM scoring system would work. I was especially fearful in the first three weeks of the quarter when many of the looks I received from teachers and students expressed ire.

In the end it did become apparent that our first efforts were beginning to pay off as I began to hear more and more students asking questions about what they needed to do in order prove they had learned the material. This was a drastic difference from the all too frequent conversations I had overheard that focused on what students needed to turn in rather than what they needed to learn.

The biggest concerns we faced at this point were: First, could we overcome the negative feelings teachers felt when they hit their first problems in making gradebook changes?

And second, what were other faculty members going to think about what we had started?

I can remember teachers who were not on the pilot team stating they would never do that and that their gradebooks belonged to them. It was clear that we had opened a Pandora's Box. I had touched a sensitive subject when I told teachers to make a change to the gradebook. The gradebook was personal. And that was something I didn't know at the time how to overcome.

We would have to work at it another year before I had a better understanding of how to bridge the gap between those who began to see a benefit and those who demanded that I stay out of their gradebooks. It was in the next year that our grading practices began to form more clearly, and the adjustments we would need in order to facilitate whole-school changes in grading practices began to emerge.

2

The First Full Year

Tony Donen
Principal

CHANGE IS A double-edged sword. On the one hand, something new creates a buzz and a sense of excitement. On the other hand, insecurity leads to fear, resistance, and for some, loathing. When our small team began analyzing our individual gradebooks, we all came to the realization that what we had been doing for many years was wrong—yet what we needed to do was unclear.

From an administrative standpoint, this is where leadership is put to the ultimate test. When the outcome is clear, managing an organization is fairly easy, and leading it is only slightly more difficult. Leading when the outcome is not clear, when the paths are plentiful, and resistance is inevitable, can be overwhelming. At this crucial transition point, the group of ten and I had to make a decision. Were we going to ignore what we had learned from our own short experiences and go back to an easier way of grading, or were we going to move forward? For me, going back was just not an option. The question became, would the group of ten keep coming with me and would more teachers dive into these unfamiliar waters of assessment?

For me, the change in our assessment practices was focused on the people. Change requires a leap of faith, and when the change begins, a leader becomes surrounded by all sorts of varied personalities.

Some people love the leap; they just leap and leap and leap and leap. I like to think of these people as a leader's starter group, "the leapers." But everyone is not so readily open to change. In fact, most don't leap so easily; they fall into other categories.

The first of the non-leapers is a group who, like the leapers, will leap—but just once. This group is like your best friend who makes fun of you. You can pester your best friend into trying anything with you—once. However, in order to get them to try the same activity a second time, you have to help them find some value in it. Otherwise they'll just tell you, "That was stupid."

These people are crucial to spreading the message that the leader is not crazy, or at the very least, that the leader's *purpose* is not crazy, even if the leader is.

Once you get past the best friends, no one likes to leap.

Most people enjoy having their feet on the ground. They will walk; you just need to ask them to walk. They're nice: they walk across campus with you at night, and they'll help you with your homework, but you have to ask them. Sometimes they don't want to walk with you, but most of the time, they will do it. The key is just to ask and to enable them to hear it from not only the leader, but also the leapers and best friends.

The most difficult group, the one that drives a leader crazy, is made up of the lifeguards. They come with a lot of preconceived ideas and rules. They don't leap; they don't walk; they sit. They blow whistles and tell others what not to do.

Lifeguards do have value because they can save you from your own stupidity. Yet, after you have been saved, it is extremely important that you get back in the water. Most of the time to accomplish that, you have to figure out how to leap or walk around the lifeguards without bringing too much attention to yourself.

If you are swimming alone, they can watch everything you do. But if you get a lot of people in the water, it becomes more difficult to stop the organization's purpose.

The reason I talk about the leapers, the best friends, the walkers, and the lifeguards is that change brings these characteristics to the forefront, and I was surrounded by people in all of these categories as we invited more and more teachers into the challenges begun by the original ten. At this crucial and early point in the process, when I determined that the results we were seeing were taking us in the right direction, I had to learn how to work with everyone. I needed to figure out which role each person in our organization was playing, specifically in the area of assessment.

In the beginning of the second year, it became clear that every teacher involved was trying to handle the challenge of what to do with assessment. I was trying to handle what to do with the people.

■

Mike Allen
U.S. and World History Teacher

WHEN I BEGAN this journey of mastery learning, I wasn't sure what to think—not because I had reservations about the concept, but because I was only in my third year of teaching at a school I loved and in the community in which I lived. So when Mr. Donen approached me to try this, I said what any eager young teacher would say: "Yes, sir."

I remember discussing the ideas of Non-Mastery, Initial Mastery, Mastery, and Advanced Mastery thinking, why on earth is there such an issue with grading? I was graded just like I grade now, and I turned out well-educated and okay.

So much of this thought process was there because I didn't know what I didn't know. It took every single bit of the time we spent discussing the intricacies of the grading scale for me to get the point: Our purpose in grading should be to assess what a student knows and doesn't know.

Even in my limited time teaching, I was frustrated with students who received A's because of extra credit. I knew kids who failed my class because they did zero homework and got B's on the tests. I have always valued personal responsibility, and homework fell under that category. There was *no way* that my homework could be a waste of time. What should the purpose of homework be, anyway? Shouldn't it be a formative assessment of the student's knowledge of content up to that point? Absolutely. But for me, it was something that students do. Period. In fact, they "did" so much of it that I had to take a day off work here and there just to grade it. And what did I grade? Completion, not accuracy, completion . . . a complete waste of time. When I moved to mastery learning, I chose my World History Honors class because I had to prepare for only one class with them, and I figured they would give me the least amount of grief. I changed our test format from being multiple choice and true/false to a strictly short-answer format. Each test had five short-answer questions that covered the entirety of the material we covered. Example question: Identify and describe the relationship between the world's two superpowers after World War II.

Their mission was to be as clear and concise as possible

in their writing, while using all of the space provided. I determined by a checklist of content points if they demonstrated Advanced Mastery, Mastery, Initial Mastery, or Non-Mastery.

- Advanced Mastery: Supported with material and relevant examples, expressing an in-depth analysis of the question.
- Mastery: Supported with material and relevant examples, but operating on the surface of the question.
- Initial Mastery: Operated on the surface of the question with limited or no support or explanation.
- Non-Mastery: Answers that appear to be guesses, offering no support or explanation.

If they demonstrated a level with which they were unhappy, the students could retest in short-answer format until they were pleased. (I believe I only retested during our lunch time and by appointment.)

Did it work? Well, sort of. It's a lot less time-consuming to mark something wrong or right than to read one hundred short answers. But did the students understand that they were going to be graded on what they *know*? Yes.

That first year really started getting my wheels turning on three main questions:

1. What is the purpose of grading?
2. What is the purpose of homework?
3. How can I help kids feel in control of their knowledge?

Another year would unfold before I had a clear vision of what that looked like.

■

Lisa Beard
Science Teacher

AS THE NEW school year began, the mastery assessment team met to discuss our successes and struggles. The collaboration helped us revise our individual assessment practices.

Once again, we all committed to implementing assessment of mastery in a minimum of one class. I chose to implement mastery in all my classes except advanced placement.

My biggest struggle from the first pilot was letting go of the numeric grading scale. I understood the significance of focusing student attention on their mastery, but I knew it would be a large leap to limit my percentage grades to 0, 70, 85, or 100 for each entry in the record book and committing to that policy for the entire school year. So, I sought a compromise.

I revisited the essential outcomes for each of my courses. Within each essential outcome, I listed all the learning objectives. Throughout the school year, unit by unit, I revised old tests and made them specific to each set of objectives.

I decided that it was important to dedicate class time after each test for students to reflect on their learning, so I wrote a corresponding self-assessment form that allowed students to track their individual levels of mastery for each set of learning objectives on the test. Students were allowed to retest any set of learning objectives.

> **Mastery example**
> Students display mastery of standards by doing work rather than writing about it or answering multiple choice questions. Sometimes they show mastery by working though a problem on their own. For instance, two learning targets might be using a multi-meter and defining Ohm's law. One assignment is to figure out how many watts a flashlight light bulb uses. I give them a multi-meter and a flashlight, and they master using a multi-meter to measure resistance; they then use that information to display mastery of Ohm's law by calculating the energy consumed by the flashlight.
>
> **George Mast**
> *Computer Teacher*

Self-assessment proved to be a break-through. Students were no longer focused on the grade at the top of their tests; rather, they were focused on what they knew and what they did not know.

By the end of the school year, I still felt like a first-year teacher. Because I chose to grade numerically, I could not figure out where homework, quizzes, and laboratory fit into the mastery approach. I allowed students to resubmit homework and reports multiple times for improved grades.

My misconception was that this improved mastery, which may or may not have been the case. Each homework "redo" was a new assignment. Each lab report was subject to multiple revisions. Each retest was customized to the student's level of mastery. And, for some reason, I chose to have quiz grades as the only type of grade that is not subject to "redos."

By the end of the school year, I realized that I was either officially insane or just had a strong desire for my students to master the essential outcomes. I knew somehow, if I were to make mastery work in my classroom, I had to come up with a more efficient way of implementation.

■

Andy Fleenor
Math Teacher

AFTER GETTING ABOUT a three-minute tutorial in my classroom from Mr. Donen during an especially raucous homeroom period, I began assessing students on a mastery scale. It was a very scaled-down version in which I graded homework for completion and graded tests and quizzes with four scores—100, 85, 70, and 0—that were broken down by specific topic. It's obvious to me now how flawed this system was, but it is also obvious how such a small change made a huge difference.

I noticed several things right away. First, overall grades plummeted to the point that nearly every student I was teaching was failing. Primarily a result of the zero grade, this situation was clearly bad and I nearly scrapped the whole thing. However, the disastrous grades began to rise quickly as students realized that fixing one small area of concern would dramatically affect their score. Students did not have to be a mathematician to realize how much better an 85 is than a 70.

> One student asked why he had to retake a quiz and before I could reply, another student said, "Because you have to really know the material."

Second, my conversations with students changed. Instead of talking about what grade a student would need on the next test to be passing, I was instead talking about what Algebra topic a student needed to master to improve her grade.

Third, grading papers became a much more simplified process. No longer did I have to mark a paper, add up the mistakes and partial credit, then change it all to a percentage. This, as any math teacher can attest, is a very time-consuming process. Instead, I merely identified how many correct questions meant a 100, an 85, or a 70 and went from there.

As time has progressed, my assessment practices too have progressed. Gone are generic quiz and test grades. Gone are grades given for completion. Gone are grades given before the student has fully learned the material. In their places are grades tied to specific skills. I am confident that a student can at any time point to his strengths as well as his weaknesses, and he can easily detail his options for better understanding.

■

Bob King
Media Teacher

AFTER TWENTY-FIVE years in business, I retired and then became a teacher. With high hopes and a little information I set out to teach media classes.

Before the school year started, my classroom had mixed seating with a dozen chairs and a dozen desk/chair combinations. I wanted only desks, but they were in short supply and unavailable for some time. When the school year started and I began teaching, quizzing, and testing, the students who had only chairs answered quizzes on their laps.

Over time I got pretty good at writing quizzes and scoring them. Grades were awarded from 0 to 100 according to how many questions a student got right. With some effort I could finish grading papers and enter grades within a day or two of each quiz.

It was distressing, though, to find that students with perfect quiz scores week after week physically could not operate our equipment. When it was time to make tape recordings, those students always waited for someone else to do the work because they couldn't or wouldn't. Students with lower quiz scores were the ones who stepped forward and operated the equipment . . . and correctly, too. It just didn't seem right.

All of the quizzing and grading seemed to miss the mark; it was a lot of busy work. I began wondering how a number grade would ensure that a student can do a job, and whether my class was really helping students prepare for the business world. It didn't feel like it. Number grades seemed arbitrary. What is the quality difference between videotapes that are graded at 93 or 95? And how are the grades important if a student can't do the work?

Todd Stinson stopped by the classroom and asked me to try something new—mastery grades. I had never heard of them, so he explained the now-familiar system in which students' work demonstrates Advanced Mastery, Mastery, Initial Mastery, or Non-Mastery.

It seemed like an easy change to make. Media students learn a variety of tasks that are very specific and very precise. Mounting a large ENG (Electronic News Gathering) video camera on a tripod is either done correctly, or is not completed. If it is done correctly the camera is firmly attached to a tripod. If it is not done correctly then the camera is not attached to the tripod and the student cannot let go of it. The grade is either "all on" (100) or "all off" (0).

Surprisingly, mastery grading has led to dramatic changes that I did not anticipate when we started using it two years ago.

It gave me the freedom to stop quizzing so often and to start observing task performance. "Could students get a high number?" was replaced by "Could they operate the equipment?"

The quizzes pretty much have been replaced by task grading. That pleased the students greatly and made the classroom seem more adult-to-adult. I changed from the "Head Parent" to a facilitator. We spend time with equipment and with how-to clinics. I spend less time checking and more time helping.

Once the quizzes went away, going paperless seemed

logical, so now the only paper we use is for storyboarding. With the paper gone, it became logical to remove the desks, so we traded them for chairs. That gave us more space and changed the atmosphere into something that feels collegial and productive. Structured rows are gone, and students sit where they please. Even better, they spend less time sitting because the atmosphere is so different that students are anxious to work with equipment.

We start class by chatting for a few minutes about today's plan. After that my job is to get out of the way, let students go to work on their projects, and help them solve problems.

More was at work here than just the change to mastery grading, but that change was a tremendous catalyst that made many things possible.

■

Valerie Willmore
Science Teacher

DURING THE SECOND year of mastery grading, I thought I would go insane keeping up with the mastery level of each student.

The hardest part was feeling like it really wasn't mastery because I kept going through objectives with everyone whether they had mastered a concept or not, but I believed that was a necessary reality with up to thirty-five students in a standard class. I felt that I spent all my spare moments filling student folders with missing labs, homework, quizzes, tests, and retakes, grading those retakes and changing grades. That was the reality, with many of the low-achieving students missing too much school and my unwillingness to write them off as another failed statistic.

The situation did calm down eventually when many of those students realized that I wasn't kidding when I told them they had to make up their work and retake tests and quizzes until they achieved at least Initial Mastery. Otherwise, they kept the Non-Mastery and an Incomplete for their overall grades. I would tease them and tell them they were going to succeed even if I had to drag them kicking and screaming the whole way, so they might as well give in and get to work.

It also helped that everyone from paraprofessionals to administrators was communicating with each other and literally hounding students about completing their missing work and retaking Non-Mastery quizzes and tests. Usually, once the student realized we weren't letting them slide through the crack and that one Non-Mastery grade changing to at least Initial Mastery made a huge impact on their grade, they succumbed and began to try. After one trimester of the process, students generally understood how it worked, and things progressed much more smoothly.

■

Jeff Myers
English Teacher

AS A RELATIVELY new English teacher, innovative ideas regarding assessment practices sounded like a great idea, even in the midst of adjusting to the other numerous facets of my career. What motivated me the most about a focus on high-quality assessment practices was the hope that providing helpful, accurate, and consistent feedback to students would encourage them to take greater ownership of their education by motivating them to revisit learning targets to improve understanding, and thus, their score.

The challenge I quickly encountered was the amount of thought, time, and planning that I needed to devote, in order to assess appropriately. For example, if a student was assessed on subject-verb agreement, she might score well when correcting lists of sentences with subject-verb agreement errors. However, when the student was given a writing assignment, her paper might be full of errors in subject-verb agreement.

Thus, a dilemma arose regarding the student's true mastery of the learning target, as well as how clearly I was defining what I wanted the student to learn. Consequently, I was forced to rethink and reword my expectations carefully.

Another challenge that arose rested in the assessment of the same learning targets in different contexts. In an English class, many learning targets are not simply taught and then never revisited throughout the rest of the year. Rather, many learning targets are assessed over and over again, especially in literature, where the theme of one work may be quite apparent, while in another work it is much more challenging to understand. Therefore, answering this question was difficult for me: If a student shows adequate understanding of the theme of one story, but shows no understanding of the theme of another story, how well does the student truly understand "theme"? I needed to consider what feedback should look like when this happened, and what the student should be required to do to clarify a true mastery of the learning target.

Despite the challenges that come with assessing a student's true knowledge of learning targets, the opportunities to engage the student in meaningful conversations about what they are learning and how they have improved is an exciting prospect. My current goal is to get students thinking more critically about what they know, what they need to improve, and what they have improved.

■

Tony Donen
Principal

IN THE FIRST full year, we began to build across the school a critical mass of teachers who believed in changing the assessment and grading process. Everyone involved, which ended up being close to half of our teachers by the end of the second year, had a slightly different take on how to change.

It became apparent that the message moving around the school was that changing our assessment and grading practices was not an option. And it wasn't even me standing up in front of the faculty saying this is not an option. (That came from me later, but not the first full year.) "This is not an option" became an unspoken message created by the roots that teachers were planting in their own practices.

My success in this first full year was in figuring out who the assessment leapers, best friends, walkers, and lifeguards were. I did not handle everyone correctly, but I was able to avoid a few lifeguards and find some best friends to help spread the purpose. In that sense, the year was a success.

George Mast wrote a great summary at the end of his first full year of moving toward a better assessment and grading practice:

> I found that I had to rewrite my labs so students could achieve Advanced Mastery on most of my assignments. It was extra work for me but improved the students' learning and encouraged the students to think more about what they were doing, and not just go through the motions. I also began to add higher-level questions at the end of the labs that encouraged analysis of the material. Mastery grading freed up my thinking about how I assessed what a student has learned.

While I was constantly concerned with the people and the overriding purpose to better our assessment and grading practices, teachers like George became concerned with the details. The first full year was truly a huge progression for our school, even though items farther down the line would seem more drastic. The first full year allowed us to build a foundation to support and further encourage the changes.

3

More Join the Team

Tony Donen
Principal

IN OUR FIRST full year of figuring out what we had started, we began to see a change in how we thought about assessment. This was not always a positive thought process or a source of pleasure, but it was a time of immense growth for many of our teachers.

The teachers working on what to do and how to do it was still an exclusive group who either were asked to try something different or took the initiative to try a new approach on their own.

So at the beginning of the second full year, we were ready to leap from exclusive to inclusive practices. We were ready to invite and encourage every teacher to dive into the water. There is only one place to dive in when it comes to assessment practices: in the set-up of the gradebook. The following chapter will focus on the specifics of setting up the gradebook and how to make the gradebook changes needed for successful assessment practices. In this chapter, however, I want to stress that this step in the process—setting up the gradebook—was the key to helping everyone take the plunge. The premise at this point in meeting our assessment challenge was to have everyone participate. And the simple modification that made everyone have to do so was in changing the categories in our gradebook.

As we moved into the school year, the staff focused on two items. The first was taking the normal categories of tests, quizzes, homework, and projects and changing them into standards, or what we called strands. So, for instance, a science teacher would no longer put Test 50%, Quizzes 30%, and Homework 20% as the categories in the gradebook. The gradebook categories had to reflect the subject matter, for example Cells 30%, Flow of Matter 30%, Heredity 40%.

This may not seem like much, but it was huge in how teachers began to think about what they assigned the students. Here are just some of the questions a teacher may have asked for one assignment given for homework:

- Did answering homework questions in Chapter 11 have anything to do with the gradebook categories?
- Did it tell the teacher anything more about what the students actual knew?
- Was this homework assignment meaningful enough to deserve a grade under the standard?

- Was the assignment a check on compliance, or did it tell us about what the student knew regarding the content?
- Did it inflate or deflate the grade inappropriately?

As many of the teachers had already dabbled in gradebook changes, the new gradebook category requirements made the efforts more consistent throughout the school. And, of course, it heightened the different personalities of the leapers, best friends, walkers, and lifeguards. At this point the conversations and questions from every group were more insightful than in the beginning. Along with the jump to change the gradebook, every teacher in school also took part in a book study of Robert Marzano's *Classroom Assessment and Grading That Works*. I selected this book for our school-wide study because it did one very important thing—it provided the key pieces of information necessary to back up the why in what we were doing. At this time in the process of changing, we knew we needed everyone to move forward and "get dirty" to some extent with the assessment and grading practices. We also knew everyone needed a clear understanding of why we were changing at all. Marzano's book does this.

We provided teachers with three options for the book study. Teachers were able to choose between reading the book on their own over the course of the year and submitting the answers to guiding questions to me. They could choose to be in a discussion group where each person was able to share ideas about the chapter of the month, or they could go to monthly presentations about each chapter.

I am not sure what this says about our school, but most people opted for the presentations. So we had Andy Fleenor, one of our math teachers who was adored and respected by other teachers, lead the presentations.

Now, one might think that Andy had some spell where he magically enamored our staff with the joys of assessment. Oh, he tried, but I can remember Andy somewhere in the middle of the year telling me that he much preferred working with teenagers. Assessment is not the most exciting topic in the world to present, and Marzano's text is certainly not the easiest work to read. However, among the options of Andy's presentations, the discussion group, and the individual readers, everyone became acutely aware of the why behind our focus. And many had their own "light bulb" moments about their personal practices at the same time.

■

Lisa Beard
Science Teacher

DURING THE SECOND full year of mastery assessment, it all came together for me.

A school-wide revamp of our current grading system was put into place. We no longer based our record-book grades on percentage points for tests, quizzes, labs, projects, and participation (which all varied teacher by teacher). Instead, we focused our percentage points on essential outcomes for the course.

For Chemistry, the record book for the first trimester reflected atomic structure, matter and energy, interactions of matter, and nuclear chemistry. The percentage assigned to these topics was based upon the time I intended to spend on these topics in class. The grade for every assignment including tests, quizzes, labs, homework, and projects was recorded in the appropriate category.

In my class, students actively participated in self-assessment after every test, and while I saw much growth and success, I still struggled with efficiency. In addition, I realized that having homework in the same category with the essential outcome was conflicting.

At the beginning of the second trimester, I tried to get a clearer picture in the record book of what each student mastered by revising my grading scale to include a homework category. Even so, I was distressed that the grades did not solely reflect mastery.

In the middle of the second trimester, I made some radical changes. I no longer graded homework, classwork, or quizzes. I merely kept a communication log that reflected checkmarks for completed homework assignments and comments for daily participation and progress. This freed my time up for tutoring, calls and e-mails to parents, and new assessments. I put the sole responsibility on the students to assess their work; and, in doing so, the assignments became something of intrinsic value and gave immediate feedback.

At first, some students took advantage of the new-found freedom. However, by the end of the trimester, one hundred percent of the students found value in doing their homework and realized the consequences of not mastering the objective meant spending many hours in lunch detention and after school until they achieved a level of mastery with which they were satisfied. The only grade reflected on the record book was the assessment grade on each of the tests.

I faced my worse fear of teaching. My students were being evaluated for what they really knew.

■

Andy Fleenor
Math Teacher

I HAVE A daughter who began competitive swimming a couple of years into the process of changing the culture of assessment at Fairview High School. Barely past swim lessons, she struggled to make it the entire length of the pool, let alone beat another swimmer.

In her first real swim meet, she swam one length of the pool in about sixty-four seconds. She finished last, was miserable, and needed some serious comforting. I put in a lot of time trying to convince her that it was less about beating other swimmers and more about showing improvement (sounds like conversations I have with students on a daily basis) and eventually she understood.

She practiced every day and attended every meet and asked to go to the pool every day for the entire summer. In her last meet she put it all together and finished her last race. She finished last, again. But her time was under thirty seconds! She had cut her original time in half—more than half—over a five-week period.

When I think about what assessment is really about, I always think about this story. If this improvement had happened in my classroom, I don't know if I can say what sort of grade she would receive. But I can say, without hesitation and with one hundred percent confidence, that she learned what was being taught to her. She attempted everything, received feedback, tried to make adjustments, received more feedback, and when it was finally time for a grade she performed well. This is my new model for assessing students in the math classroom.

It is amazing how logical this approach is, and how wrong our approach had been for so long. I began my teaching career by grading the same way I was graded in high school. The only reason I did it that way was that's all I knew. But in real life, who wants to be assessed that way?

If I have a bad day teaching a troublesome bunch of

teenagers, I don't want to have to spend the rest of the year being perfect to help cancel out one bad performance. When I am reviewed by my principal, I don't want the comment, "Good lesson." No, I want specifics on what went well and what didn't go well.

And perhaps most important, I don't want to know after the job is complete that I am doing a terrible job. I want to know while I'm working so I can make changes. Students—and teachers, reporters, engineers, pilots, truck drivers—will perform their tasks better when given specific feedback about strengths and weaknesses and specific suggestions to improve performance.

As teachers we have no choice about giving numerical grades, but we owe it to our students to go beyond the number.

■

Tiffany Johnson
English Teacher

I'LL BE HONEST; I still didn't like the system we worked out, but the good news is that my story had a happy ending.

Yes, I still heard the teachers who said, "If it isn't for a grade, then they aren't going to do it." I somewhat agreed with that, but I had also seen kids doing work that wasn't for a grade because they knew if they didn't know it by the test day or final draft day, not only would they have to do the assignment again, on their own time, but they would also suffer other consequences.

I understood why an average may not be the best way to assess students, because that was just a number, not a scale of knowledge. In addition, I was able to try other things. I did not have to be married to AM, M, IM, NM, which made me happy. I had switched to a 1–5 grade scale for many assignments. An example of a 1–5 paper is displayed in Figure 3-1 adapted from part of an Advanced Placement rubric.

Of course, the kids still wanted to change that into a percentage, but I didn't make it a percentage. In my class, a 4/5 was not usually equal to an 80. At the same time, a 3/5 may have been a 70 instead of a 60. What I was striving for was consistency for each assignment. I recorded assignments in a paper gradebook. Then when it was time to put grades in, I went back and looked at two things:

1. Did the student show improvement?
2. Were the scores always about the same?

Using this information, I felt confident that the number I put in the gradebook was fair, represented what the student knew, and was based on several chances given to that student.

Figure 3-1 is a table with three sections: Fluency and Originality, Idea Development and Evidence, and Vocabulary/Grammar. It shows descriptions for rankings 1 through 5.

Fig. 3-1: Gradebook rankings

Fluency and Originality

1 Often described as vague or simple. The essay may be one paragraph. These essays are unacceptable and boring. Yawn.

2 There is no ease of writing. I expect more originality from a college-bound student.

3 There is some consistency in style and fluency among the paragraphs. These essays are acceptable but not impressive. Generally speaking, these essays are superficial. In other words, "Where's the WOW?"

4 The paper has some fluency. The style is fairly consistent. These essays are proficient. Lacking WOW, but still good.

5 All paragraphs are linked for a fluid, cohesive paper. WOW! The style is readable and consistent. These essays are clearly outstanding. The essays offer creative and original ideas and insights that are extensively elaborated and refreshing.

Idea Development and Evidence

1 The essay summarizes or makes the most general observations of the text. This essay has little evidence of textual support or the support does not relate to a clear purpose.

2 The ideas are not developed. The essay offers little or no textual evidence (although there may be a summary).

3 The analysis tends to border on summary, thus the writer offers quoted material or textual information in place of analysis. The conclusion only summarizes main points and/or the thesis.

4 The ideas are developed, but there may be problems with the textual examples. The essays refer to the texts, explicitly or implicitly, but offer less detailed or less convincing explanations, or less sufficient development. More often, the quotes are not blended into the analysis. The conclusion provides summary rather than insight.

5 These essays go beyond general commentary, referring to the texts, explicitly or implicitly, offering specific details, blending quotes where appropriate. They offer compelling connections between technique and effect. The conclusion provides an insightful ending to the essay.

Vocabulary and Grammar

1 Serious errors in sentence structure, paragraphing, transition, punctuation, and vocabulary.

2 Although the writer's idea may be conveyed, the essay does not demonstrate control of sentence variety, punctuation, vocabulary, verb choice, or focus.

3 The writer should focus more on revision: topic sentences, sentence variety, redundancy, punctuation, weak verbs, wordiness, transition, vocabulary.

4 Although the essay may be mechanically accurate, more attention should be given to sentence variety, precise vocabulary, active verbs, and focus.

5 The writer makes use of sophisticated vocabulary, sentence variety, parallel structure, modification. The language is concise and lucid, verbs active, and punctuation is effective.

■

Mike Allen
U.S. and World History Teacher

IN MY SECOND year I had a much clearer vision for my assessment practices. I remember so vividly the days of breathing that sigh of relief when it was test day, because I worked so doggedly hard during the previous two weeks: grading worksheets, trying to fill time, getting through the material, and so on.

When I realized that I was pursuing grading for all the wrong reasons, I felt a weight lift off my shoulders. What if I worked on communicating the purpose of the class and built all my formative assessments based on clearly communicating that purpose? What if I pursued the content with the clear focus of the expectation of knowledge, and then graded the students purely on what they can prove that they have learned? What a revolution!

I still read that and say "YES!" out loud because it makes so much more sense.

I expanded my initial jaunt into mastery learning by using it with my standard United States History courses as well as my standard World History course. I dropped the essay-only format in favor of a direction that our school was moving regarding the standards. The Tennessee History Standards have six different categories: Culture, Geography, Economics, Governance and Civics, History, and Individuals, Groups, and Interactions. I found it very difficult to objectively separate the assessment questions on the test into the six categories. I found it even more difficult to explain to a student, "I'm sorry. It looks like you didn't understand Culture." What does that even mean to an adult, let alone a teenager?

By my third year, I was able to streamline my categories to align with the U.S. History standards in a way that was accessible to the students. When my students are assessed now, they have different categories under one strand that help them comprehend what they do and don't understand.

Once a progress report is received, a student can do a "Prove-It" session. If a student believes that he can show me that he has learned about urban growth during the turn of the nineteenth century, shouldn't he receive credit for having learned it? Isn't that the point of a class, to show what you've learned? When the student comes to my room, he needs a blank sheet of paper and the "Prove-It" questions (Figure 3-2). If he can accurately answer the questions, he gets credit for his knowledge. If he can't, he does not receive credit. It's a beautiful moment: Assessing kids based on what they know!

Fig. 3-2: Prove-It Questions

US HISTORY – ALLEN
1.2: Industrial Growth and the Gilded Age
Urban Growth

1. From the end of the Civil War until the beginning of the 20th century, what happened to the size of cities?
2. Why did people leave their farms and migrate to the cities?
3. During the late 19th century, the greatest urban growth was found in what regions of America?
4. What were a few problems presented by immigration?
5. Define immigration.
6. Define urban growth.
7. Define ethnic ghettos.
8. Define nativism.
9. For each of the following characteristics, you must decide if they more accurately describe immigration before the Civil War (B) or after the Civil War (A).
   __They were often accepted as Protestant whites.
   __They were culturally and religiously different than native-born Americans.
   __They were increasingly Jewish.
   __Most immigrants came from Eastern and Southern Europe.
   __They were generally accepted.
   __Most immigrants came from Western Europe.
   __They were culturally and religiously similar to native-born Americans.

■

Valerie Willmore
Science Teacher

MY GOAL FOR the year was changing the grading scale to a 1–4 system, focusing on tests along with involving students in the assessment process. Unfortunately, the grading program required these points to be translated into a number. So, 4 = 100%, 3 = 85%, 2 = 75%, and 1 = F or Incomplete.

Until this point my focus had been on the essential concepts to assess for my class. Now it was time to get the students more involved in comprehending why they got the score they did on tests. Therefore, they completed a self-assessment check list while they took their tests to indicate their understanding level of each question (guessed, knew it, not sure) and then again when their tests were returned to indicate why a question was missed (right, wrong, simple mistake, didn't know it, I need to restudy).

Each test also had a cover sheet that indicated the strand and learning target being assessed, along with a grading rubric. Students looked through their tests and determined why their scores were 1, 2, 3, or 4. This information was kept on a master assessment chart in a student assessment folder in my room. Not only did I have a good idea of what each student knew or didn't know, but they had a good idea also from charting their progress.

I knew I was going the right direction when a small huddle of students surrounded my desk to find out how to improve their grades. One student asked why they had to retake a quiz and before I could reply, another student said, "Because you have to really know the material." Eureka! What a concept! Know the information and what it really means. I knew I had some bugs to work out, but I was hooked on the fact that I knew what each student really understood about physical science concepts.

More importantly, the biggest change I noticed was in the confidence level of students: Most of the low-achieving students really liked it. Some had never seen many passing grades, let alone A's, B's or C's. They felt a sense of accomplishment because they on their own could succeed and didn't need to rely on someone else for their grades. They also didn't feel down-trodden with a Non-Mastery because they knew they could try again.

Bob King
Media Teacher

TO ANY TEACHER it feels like payday when a student says, "I love this class."

The change to mastery grading helped me move away from the boring routine of frequent quizzes and all that goes with them: last-minute prep sessions so students could avoid low grades, anxiety for some, classroom rules imposed during quiz time, lots of paper, and lots of grading.

At first the change created a void. With all the quiz-related stuff gone, what would I do with the extra time?

The very simple answer became clear over several months--focus on the standards. What are the basic standards that students are to learn, and how do we get at them most directly?

I recently rewrote my grading criteria for the fourth time in five years. I really wanted to focus on the basic standards. Could students set up camera controls for a shot? Could they tell a video story effectively? Could they light a subject properly? These are things that would prepare them to work in this field if they wished to do so. They still needed to learn about connectors, and coiling cables, and many other things, but we no longer tested on those because they were small steps to larger things.

Students and I discovered we could do things that are a little more complex, a little more sophisticated, and a lot more enjoyable than before. We spent less time on little tasks and more time on the final product. The students enjoyed the work more, so they needed less supervision and earned more autonomy. Better, we built relationships that were based on a higher level of trust and common interest with each other. I spent less time making them do things that seemed academic. They spent less time disliking it and more time learning.

Perhaps the best benefit was that students said, "I love this class" a lot more often.

■

Tony Donen
Principal

THE PREVIOUS CHAPTER showed you how we laid the foundation for change at our school, and in this chapter teachers have shared the effects of the change that we saw in the first full year of implementation. This included teachers' modifying the mastery grading scale (NM, IM, M, AM) to suit their classroom needs.

The change took the entire year, the Marzano book study, and more modifications of the gradebook categories before we saw our efforts begin to pay off. Change also created a sense of purpose throughout the faculty, doing what we were doing even if there was not a clear end. We collectively knew why, and we collectively knew that we needed to spend a lot more time on the what.

We had plenty of snares that year but one of the largest came with our special education population. Kathy Martin, a special education teacher, best sums it up:

> My concern about special education students and the concept of mastery learning is that many of our students have severe cognitive disabilities. Our district has a policy of full inclusion for our special

> education students. Many students prior to implementing mastery learning have "passed" a class through sheer effort. Compliance and completion have been a large part of their grades.
>
> Mastery concentrates on what they learn. Sometimes what they are asked to learn is beyond them. Many have memory issues. Special education teachers and assistants can use the IEP and accommodation strategies to scaffold the work to meet the student's level. And during the year, there were questions raised on what help special education students really should receive. These were difficult conversations, but we ended up in a place where teachers became more familiar with the accommodations, how to better grade students with IEP's, and how accommodations play a role in all students learning.

Our special education dilemma was very challenging as many of the grades associated with "trying hard" began to be replaced by performance level. However, the conversations, tears, flexibility, and understanding of student needs turned out to be a process we needed to experience. The change was not easy, and we didn't answer all of the questions, yet we began asking many of the right questions about each student's learning and how we assess that learning.

In a nutshell, four principles became clear over the course of our trials:

- Assessment and grading are tied directly to each other.
- Schools, administrators, and teachers are experts in content, knowledgeable in instructional delivery, and novices in assessment.
- "Leapers" are great in starting change, but "best friends" are crucial to the success of making change a reality.
- The gradebook is the crucial piece in changing the culture of your school and reporting what the school values.

4

Traditional Gradebook: Case Studies

Tony Donen
Principal

AT THIS POINT in the grading and assessment process, you are probably wondering about the student. So, what happens if I make these changes? Show me the effect standards-based grading will have on my students. In order to do just that, we have provided three student examples for you in this chapter. We believe you know these students, even if the names are different for you. Let's meet Tommy, Jennifer, and Andy.

Comments from their teachers:

JENNIFER'S TEACHER: Oh no, here comes Jennifer again. That kid drives all the adults here crazy. It would be nice if I could come to school one time, just one time, and see Jennifer actually doing something to meet her potential. She never brings her materials to class, jokes about not doing her homework, and, honestly, makes me wonder why I am teaching.

TOMMY'S TEACHER: Here comes Tommy. It's always a guessing game on how well he is going to do on my tests. I just cannot get a good read on him. I sometimes wonder who is helping him on his homework. But overall, he's just a nice kid, and I really like having him in class. When it comes to class work, Tommy does everything I ask him to do.

ANDY'S TEACHER: Andy? Never says much. Yeah, pretty typical kid. If the normal curve still existed, you know, that one that has a certain amount of A, B, C, D, and F grades, he would be smack in the center. I usually try to pace my lessons and activities for the middle so that helps Andy out. But, I also feel bad for him because he doesn't get much of my attention. Could he do better? Oh yeah, but he is pretty much compliant so what else can I expect? With thirty students in that class, it is hard to cater to everyone's needs.

All the kids in your classes are unique, but we also have all taught Jennifer, Tommy, and Andy. In this chapter and those that follow, it is our goal for you to experience what happens with them as you move away from a traditional grading and assessment system to a standards-based system similar to the one delineated in the previous chapter. Let us start with three traditional progress reports for each of these students in the areas of math, science and language arts (English class).

Jennifer: Traditional Progress Report #1

Student: **Jennifer** Average: **70.68%**
Class: **Pre-calculus**

Tests and Projects 40%		
Assignment	**Points Possible**	**Points Earned**
Chapter 1 Test	100	88
Chapter 4 Test	100	92
Chapter 5 Test	100	97
Transformations Project	100	87
	Category Average: **91.00%**	

Quizzes 30%		
Assignment	**Points Possible**	**Points Earned**
Chapter 1 Quiz A	100	90
Chapter 1 Quiz B	100	97
Chapter 4 Quiz A	100	99
Chapter 4 Quiz B	100	94
Chapter 5 Quiz A	100	90
Chapter 5 Quiz B	100	88
	Category Average: **93.00%**	

Homework 30%		
Assignment	**Points Possible**	**Points Earned**
Chapter 1 Homework: 10 assignments	100	40
Chapter 4 Homework: 10 assignments	100	10
Chapter 5 Homework: 10 assignments	100	0
Participation	100	35
	Category Average: **21.25%**	

When asked to describe Jennifer, what are the initial impressions you get from the progress report? When this was given to a group of teachers at a conference, the answers were downright scary. I wondered if any of us should be in teaching at all, but here is the cleaned up version. According to conference attendees, Jennifer seems . . .

> *"lazy"*
> *"bored"*
> *"lacking in ambition"*
> *"too cool for school"*
> *"rebellious"*

and she . . .

> *"probably has parents that can't handle her"*
> *"hates all adults"*

. . . and the list goes on and on; thankfully, there is always a positive side that gets thrown out there—Jennifer is a good test-taker, some say, and others believe she seems to know what she is doing. Unfortunately, whatever it is that she knows we cannot necessarily define.

JENNIFER: That teacher just doesn't like me. I don't get why I have to do any of the work assigned. It's obvious I can do it. You know, it's just easier to skip that class. The teacher is happy when I am not there. I certainly am. And who cares? I'm passing the class, and I show up for her dumb quizzes and tests.

JENNIFER'S MOM: I can't wait until she is out of school. I just don't understand why she has to always play with fire. Jennifer never brings home any work. If I have to have one more meeting with her teachers, I'll lose it. When the school calls, I have gotten so used to it that I just go numb when I answer the phone.

Tommy: Traditional Progress Report #2

Student: **Tommy**
Class: **Biology**

Average: **84.00%**

Tests and Projects 40%		
Assignment	**Points Possible**	**Points Earned**
Chapter 1-2 Test	100	68
Chapter 3-4 Test	100	79
Chapter 5-6 Test	100	74
Project	100	95
	Category Average:	**79.00%**

Quizzes 30%		
Assignment	**Points Possible**	**Points Earned**
Chapter 1 Quiz	100	55
Chapter 2 Quiz	100	80
Chapter 3 Quiz	100	74
Chapter 4 Quiz	100	75
Chapter 5 Quiz	100	88
Chapter 6 Quiz	100	65
	Category Average:	**74.40%**

Homework 30%		
Assignment	**Points Possible**	**Points Earned**
Chapter 1 Homework	100	100
Chapter 2 Homework	100	100
Chapter 3 Homework	100	100
Chapter 4 Homework	100	100
Chapter 5 Homework	100	100
Participation	100	100
	Category Average:	**100.00%**

What are your initial impressions of Tommy? At first,

many people look at the homework and quickly say, "I love this kid." Then, about two seconds later, after looking at the quiz and test grades, comments become less and less positive and appreciative. Comments include items such as Tommy . . .

"is probably copying his homework"
"obviously can do the work"
"doesn't know how to study"
"is a bad test taker"
"is working at his potential"
"is doing just the best he can do"
"is lucky to have an 84—so everyone should be happy"

. . . and so forth.

TOMMY: Everyone knows I am not a straight A student, but an 84 is really pretty good. Heck, I have a higher grade than half the students in class, and they all think they know more than me. I like the way the teacher does his grades. It really helps me, especially that project, because I am not the best test-taker, but I am organized and can get my work done.

TOMMY'S DAD: We have always preached work ethic in our household. If Tommy doesn't do his work, you let me know, and I'll take care of it. Tommy has around a 3.0 GPA, and we let him know that is good. We expect him to go to college and do well. Tommy's a good kid; he has done well from kindergarten to high school.

Andy: Traditional Progress Report #3

Student: **Andy**
Class: **English 10**

Average: **86.00%**

Tests and Projects 40%

Assignment	Points Possible	Points Earned
Chapter 1 Parts of Speech	100	88
Chapter 4 Phrases and Clauses	100	77
Chapter 5 Sentence Correction	100	89
Research Paper	100	98
	Category Average:	**88.00%**

Quizzes 30%

Assignment	Points Possible	Points Earned
Chapter 1 Quiz 1	100	78
Chapter 1 Quiz 2	100	69
Chapter 4 Quiz 1	100	70
Chapter 5 Quiz 1	100	88
Dante's Inferno Quiz 1	100	90
Dante's Inferno, Quiz 2	100	92
	Category Average:	**79.00%**

Homework/Classwork 30%

Assignment	Points Possible	Points Earned
Research Notes	100	100
Literature Notes	100	80
Grammar Notes	100	80
Vocabulary Assignment 1	100	90
Vocabulary Assignment 2	100	100
1st Draft Research Paper Completed	100	100
Participation	100	90
	Category Average:	**90.00%**

Andy is the typical kid. Andy seems to be doing all right. He is fairly compliant, appears to be performing probably a little bit better in English class than the average student, and he really knocked out that research paper. With all the kids they have in class, teachers appreciate how Andy helps out the teacher in managing the class. He doesn't stand out, in either direction, and that really helps the teacher and the class to be able to keep moving forward. He'll be fine.

ANDY: Class is class. English is not my favorite subject, but I can do it all right. I don't cause any problems in class, and I am more than happy with my grade. Best part is I don't have to worry either way about the teacher singling me out. I blend in pretty well, and, as long as I keep a low profile, everyone will leave me alone.

ANDY'S MOM: Both Andy's dad and I work full-time jobs. We really don't hear much, if anything, from the school, and when we get his report card, everything looks fine. Andy is just a normal kid, likes his music, answers "fine" when we do ask about how school is going, and we even think he has a girlfriend (even though he would hate for us to meet her). We don't really worry about him.

■

In each scenario with Jennifer, Tommy, and Andy, it is important to note the emphasis of the language used by the student, the teacher, and the parent. The emphasis is not on learning. The emphasis is on behavior. We can tell you a number of facts about the student in terms of student behavior. However, we have very little understanding and even less communication regarding what a student knows, what the student does not know, and what the student experiences as strengths or weaknesses in terms of content learning.

Learning is the most important piece of education. The way the traditional gradebook is arranged primarily communicates information about behavior only. There is little being communicated about what students are to know and be able to do with the subject. All three students have one thing in common: they have all received grades using a traditional grading system, but they don't have a clue what specific objectives they have achieved. And, thus, helping students learn and grow falls squarely back to which students can be the most compliant. This is the main reason we believed our grading practices needed a major overhaul. The most common-sense approach was revamping the gradebook to reflect how students were mastering the standards of each course. It was time to take a dive into restructuring the gradebook.

5

Categories and Assignments

PHILOSOPHICALLY, WE BELIEVE that every teacher, administrator, student, and parent agrees, at least holistically, that students should be assessed on what they know. Also, we believe that student grades should reflect what the student knows.

In elementary school, standards-based reporting makes sense. We can give students and parents a list of skills that students should be working toward, and then check the skills off as they are mastered. In kindergarten through second grade, parents and teachers are even comfortable with grading systems that expand beyond "yes" and "no," and provide students with a level of progress toward a skill. There are also plenty of examples of leveled grading in the primary grades in which parents receive feedback on a student's progress over time. In fact, as a parent we get excited when our child brings home a first-grade report card that has a one to four grading system for different skills. It allows us to recognize and applaud our child's strengths, assist with weaker areas, and follow growth across the year.

Yet, you may wonder how this applies to middle school and high school. Regardless of how you change your assessment practices, the reality is that students in high school are going to receive transcripts that have grades on them. Colleges and universities are accustomed to receiving cumulative course grades; they are not interested in the details indicating whether a student received a two in poetry analysis and a four in determining the tone of a writer. This seems to beg the question, how do I convert standards-based grading to a gradebook that reports the cumulative course grade?

In this chapter, we will begin to float ideas to you for reporting a grade that reflects mastery of material. The final grade will be a number like those you are accustomed to seeing and using. However, the process used to get the number has changed. The reporting of progress throughout a grading period has changed. We are not advocating that cumulative course grades become obsolete; once a student has completed his high school program of study, the courses that the student chose to take in high school will have a grade attached to them. What we believe is that this grade should communicate a student's strengths and weaknesses. The gradebook organization will impact how the grade is reported and calculated.

■

After making the very important decision to change the assessment practices in your school or classroom, you have to decide how you are going to record the grades. Teachers are accustomed to categorizing student grades based on the type of assessment given (*i.e.*, homework, quizzes, tests, projects, labs, etc.). Instead of creating categories based on the type of assessment given, create categories that reflect state standards, the titles of units being taught, or some other logical grouping of course content.

In Tennessee, all high school math courses are divided into five identical state standards. These standards are:

1.) Mathematical processes
2.) Numbers and operation
3.) Algebra
4.) Geometry and measurement
5.) Data analysis and probability.

In the math department, these five standards are the gradebook categories. Everything assessed should fit into one of these categories. By changing the organization of the gradebook, the ambiguous entry "Chapter 2 Test" does not make sense. The test must be titled something descriptive about what is being assessed on the test. Not only should a student be able to look at a progress report and know her "grade," the student should also be able to look at the report and know her strengths and weaknesses. A student's knowledge that she does not understand Chapter 2 is not helpful in giving feedback to the student on what she can work on to improve her knowledge. It is much more beneficial to the student to see the assignment "solving equations" as an entry on a progress report. This way the student knows that she needs help understanding the target of solving equations.

It would also be appropriate to divide the assignment into sections to enter it into the gradebook. For the previously mentioned example, the assignments entered in the gradebook could be one-step equations, two-step equations, equations with variables on both sides, and equations involving parentheses. After grades are entered into the appropriate assignment, a student can look at a progress report and understand exactly where he is having trouble. As a teacher, this is helpful when a student comes in for extra help as there is a definite direction in which to proceed. The guesswork is gone. Teachers no longer have to spend time distinguishing between what a student thinks he does not understand and exactly where a student needs to focus; this way, more time can be spent on reteaching and helping. To a parent, the feedback from this gradebook organization is much more descriptive than 67% on a "Chapter 2 Test." Furthermore, the student can use a gradebook categorized in this manner as feedback to guide further study.

Gradebook reorganization has two main components:

Component 1:

Change the categories in the gradebook to reflect standards or units.

Example 1: Pre-Calculus Gradebook Categories

Functions and Graphs	15%
Trigonometric Functions	40%
Analytical Trigonometry	45%

This gradebook is for one grading period of Pre-Calculus. It is clear from the percentages that the focus of the grading period is trigonometry.

Example 2: US History Categories

Industrial Development and the Late Nineteenth Century	35%
The Emergence of Modern America	35%
The Great Depression	30%

The history teacher decided that time periods or units were the categories he wanted to use in dividing his gradebook. Percentages are based on the amount of time in the grading period spent in the particular unit.

Example 3: English III Categories

Literature and Research	15%
Literature and Informational Text	40%
Writing and Research	45%

This gradebook utilizes the categories our state mandates as learning standards for Language Arts. The categories which include the word "and" consist of two state standards which are taught together in the context of the course.

Example 4: Chemistry Categories

Matter and Energy	10%
Periodic Table and Trends	15%
Mathematics of Chemical Equations	30%
Chemical and Nuclear Energy	30%
Chemical Bonding	15%

This gradebook has state standards as categories. The percentages are based on the time focused in the particular area during the grading period.

Depending on the gradebook program used at your particular school, your categories might need to include a final exam, and the percentages will need to be adjusted to reflect the exam as well.

Component 2:

Change the names of the assignments entered in the gradebook to reflect skills or processes assessed.

We are now going to illustrate one of the aforementioned

categories for each of the subjects. The assignments are input into the gradebook in a way that the assignment type is indicated as well as the learning target or concept.

Example 5: Pre-Calculus Gradebook Category and Assignments

Analytic Trigonometry 45%
Quiz 1: Verifying Trig Identities
Quiz 2: Law of Sines
Quiz 2: Law of Cosines
Test 1: Verifying Trig Identities
Test 1: Law of Sines
Test 1: Law of Cosines

Notice how the teacher gave a quiz over one learning target (Verifying Trig Identities), a separate quiz over two learning targets that were entered as two separate grades. The teacher also gave one test in this unit over three learning targets, and the test was entered as three separate grades.

Example 6: US History Assignments

Industrial Development and the Late 19th Century 35%
Test 1: War's Impact on Industrialism
Test 1: Disparity Among Groups
Test 1: Western Migration
Test 1: Grand Administration
Test 2: Urban vs. Rural
Test 2: Urban Growth
Test 2: Impact of Western Expansion
Project: Industry Leaders Presentation

The US History teacher gave two tests during the unit over the Industrial Revolution and the Late Nineteenth Century. Each test covered several learning targets; the tests were each entered as multiple assignments into the gradebook according to the learning target assessed. There is also a project in the unit entered as its own separate grade.

Example 7: English III Assignments

Writing and Research 45%
Quiz: Note-taking and Prewriting Strategies
Test 1: Thesis Statement and Outline
Research Paper: First Draft
Research Paper: First Revision— Proofreading and Rewriting
Test 2: MLA Format and Source Citation
Research Paper: MLA Format and Source Citation

In English, the research paper is divided into many assignments. Initially there is a quiz covering one learning target, Note-taking and Prewriting Strategies. There are two different tests covering separate learning targets of research paper elements. The actual research paper is entered as separate assignments in the gradebook depending on the part of the research paper being assessed.

Example 8: Chemistry Assignments

Chemical and Nuclear Energy 30%
Lab Report I: Types of Chemical Reactions
Lab Report II: Activity Series of Metals
Test 1: Balancing Chemical Equations
Test 2: Synthesis and Decomposition
Test 2: Combustion
Test 2: Single Replacement and Double Replacement

> In chemistry, there is one test covering one learning target, a second test covering three learning targets entered as three separate assignments, and two lab reports each entered as their own assignment.

In each of the examples above the assignment in each particular category is descriptive, telling the teacher, student, and parent exactly the focus of the assessment. This is designed so that by looking at the gradebook, the strong and weak areas can be identified clearly. The quick identification of these areas allows teachers and students to focus remediation immediately. The purpose of a gradebook is to effectively communicate progress and achievement. Through clear categories that reflect standards or units and through descriptive assignments that reflect skills or processes assessed, meaningful communication occurs.

6

How We Made Changes

GRADEBOOKS CAN LOOK different for different classes that you teach.

If you teach more than one type of class during the day, the gradebook for each could look drastically different from class to class and still accomplish the same goal. Remember, the goal is that grades and grade reports reflect mastery of material in a course. The method used in achieving this goal differs from class to class. Dr. Thomas Guskey, widely known for his education reform research, supports this in an article for *Educational Leadership* (1994), "No one method of grading and reporting serves all purposes well."

Each class taught has different goals and different standards. There is no perfect gradebook for every situation; teachers must determine the best gradebook to communicate student achievement separately for each class they teach. For example, daily activities in one class may receive scores even if these do not go into the gradebook; while in a different class these scores might be tracked in the gradebook without impacting the overall grade in order to monitor preliminary assignments or daily work. In still other classes, particularly honors classes, daily work may not need to be marked or tracked for the students to be motivated. And when it comes to determining the category labels you want to use in the gradebook, state standards can be used as categories in one class while unit topics are used in another. As a teacher, you have to decide what organization of the gradebook works best for your class and your students.

Final grades demand the use of professional judgment

Using a standards-based grading system involves professional judgment in final grade determinations. Straightforward number-crunching, percentages, means, and medians do not accurately reflect mastery toward a target. Computers cannot accurately give a student a grade that reflects achievement of a standard or skill. Robert J. Marzano describes "the power law of learning" in *Classroom Assessment and Grading that Works* (2006). The principle behind "the power law of learning," introduced by researchers Newell and Rosenbloom, explains that a true representation of student learning can be successfully estimated. Marzano goes even further to explain that using an average maintains that every attempt by a student to demonstrate mastery of a learning target would be the same. Student learning, in fact, would be the same from the beginning to the end of a grading period.

The power law is based on the idea that student learning grows over time. Every student's grade should be determined through several opportunities to perform a skill. Achievement should be looked at as a whole, not the average of the performances. The goal is mastery of the material or of the skill. Many failing attempts at the skill do not, in fact, demand a failing grade. If a teacher observes growth toward the achievement of the target during the course of the grading period, then the teacher should account for the level of target mastery in the final grade.

Yes, even if the student miserably "failed" the test the first time, the student should be given credit for mastering the skill when he masters it. The student grade should reflect the mastery more than the failure. All scores do not have to count, especially in situations where steady progress is made toward mastery of the target, or in a situation in which mastery of the target is ultimately achieved. Exceptionally good scores should also not be counted if the student does not know how to reproduce that level of mastery at a later date. While the power law may confirm the results shown by your grades, it is crucial that you use professional judgment in determining final grades for your students.

Converting rubric scores to gradebook entries

Many of our teachers who used rubrics in their grading struggled when translating those scores into the gradebook entry. In *Converting Rubric Scores to Grades*, a presentation at the Sound Grading Practices Conference in 2008, Judy Arter, a leader in performance assessment, clarified how to utilize rubrics effectively. The following examples are based on a system proposed and explained in that presentation:

A direct conversion to percents would look like this:

5 out of 5 = 100%

4 out of 5 = 80%

3 out of 5 = 60%

2 out of 5 = 40%

1 out of 5 = 20%

It does not seem reasonable that out of the five possibilities for scores, there are three F's, one C, and one A. The teacher should use logic (and professional judgment) to determine the number that is entered into the gradebook. For example, the following conversion provides a good basis for many teachers who give a single overall rubric grade for an assignment:

Points out of 5	Numeric Grade	Letter Grade
5	100	A
4	88	B
3	76	C
2	65	F
1	50	F

For assignments with many different traits, a conversion table such as this can be utilized:

Rubric Scores	Overall Grade
Half the scores are 5's, no more than one is below 4	95 / A
Half the scores are 4's or 5's, no more than one is below 3	85 / B
Half the scores are 3's or better, no more than one is below 2	75 / C
Half the scores are 2's or better, no more than two are below 2	70 / D
Three or more scores are below 2	60 / F

The key to converting rubric scores to grades is to use a method that you as the teacher understand and think is fair. You must be able to communicate these grades to students and parents, who will, undoubtedly, have questions. These conversions must fit into your class and your assignment and may vary from class to class and from assignment to assignment. Whichever method you choose, be sure to share your conversion table with students when initially discussing the assignment.

Dangerous waters to avoid

Extra Credit. It is difficult to escape the topic of extra credit when discussing students' grades. This is especially true as you near the end of a grading period when parents and students often inquire about ways to improve the student's overall grade. Over the years many types of extra credit have been used with varying degrees of validity, from dressing up on special days, to attending after-school activities, to reading and completing a report on a book not covered during class time. *Only* academic achievement should be communicated through a student's grade—extra credit, therefore, should not find its way into our gradebooks.

A better solution is to provide students with additional opportunities to prove what they have learned and mastered. A good illustration of this is a variation of an example give by Ken O'Connor, aka The Grade Doctor, in his book *A Repair Kit for Grading* (2007). Let's suppose a student scores a 60%, 75%, 65%, 81%, 85%, and an 84% on the first six assessments. If calculated in a traditional way, this student would have a 75% and receive a grade of C. The student completes three extra credit assignments (which may or may not be related to learning targets) worth two points each, and ends up with an average of 81% and receives a B. If we are honest with ourselves, we all see that the final grade does not accurately reflect the student's mastery of the content.

Instead consider the same student above, with the same assessment grades. The teacher offers to allow the student to replace the three lowest scores by retaking similar assessments (or parts of similar assessments). The student scores a 75%, an 82%, and a 79%, bringing the overall average, once again, to an 81%. This time, however, we are more confident that the student's level of achievement is communicated. This is not simply adding points to the student's grade; it is allowing the student to prove that mastery of a topic has grown.

Zeros. Another difficult hurdle to overcome in this progression is avoiding the use of zeros. At first glance it may seem unrealistic to never use a grade of zero for a student. Standard procedure for many teachers has been to assign a grade of zero when a student failed to turn in an assignment. This, however, does not fit our philosophy of grading. Thomas Guskey (2005), among others, advocates the use of "Incomplete" rather than assigning a zero. We think that if a student fails to turn in an assignment, no numeric grade should be given. The student should be made to turn in the assignment (even if it is past the due date) with no penalty to his grade. We are not saying that there should be no consequence, only that his grade should be based on achievement. We view turning in work late or doing no work at all as a behavior issue requiring a behavior consequence. One possible consequence is to assign students to a detention period in which the student can complete assignments and get remediation help if needed.

Adrift at sea

Work Habits. Every teacher understands what work habits are, but many do not understand how including work habits interferes with the communication of content mastery. Some examples (though there are many others) of grades that depend on work habits are as follows: grades based on completion of an assignment, grades giving points for being prepared for class, grades taking away points for being late or unprepared, grades taking away points for being absent. Other consequences of work habits that may be shown include not accepting work that was completed and correct but not on time, counting off points for late work, and not taking work because a student absence was unexcused.

Student work habits are important. It is essential that students learn accountability, punctuality, turning in work on time, preparedness, and completion as habits vital to survival; however, in a standards-based grading system, there is no place for these habits to be figured into the grade calculation. In *Measuring and Evaluation in the Classroom* (1990), J.R. Hills says that:

> [T]he primary function of grading and marking is to communicate effectively to a variety of audiences the degree of achievement of academic competence of individual students. . . . And it is unethical to use a low grade as a form of punishment because to do so is dishonest. The grade should be an accurate and meaningful summary of the level to which a student has learned what he was being taught, such as science or spelling, not deportment or promptness or

> conformity—and that summary should not be distorted by motivational or other considerations.

Many teachers, those at our school included, have a very hard time letting work habits go. The argument is that if these habits don't count in the grade, then the student will not learn the lesson. How then can students still be taught good work habits when work habits are not graded?

One way is through behavioral punishments for behavioral actions. If a student is unprepared, a teacher can assign a detention. Completed work is not a reflection of mastery of a topic. Students can be assigned homework, but grading the work on completion alone does not at all reflect what the student is able to do with respect to the learning target. Homework should be given for one of three reasons: to be marked for accuracy of work completed, feedback of movement toward mastery of a learning target, or practice of a skill newly learned.

Some teachers have dealt with work habits at our school is by making homework the only way to be allowed a retest. Students who do poorly on an assessment have the opportunity to retake the assessment. Note that this is an opportunity, not a right. Students must show that they have done the work necessary to understand a concept better than they did, before they are allowed to retake an assessment or part of an assessment. Students who wish to retake must show that they have attempted all the homework associated with the particular learning target, and then they must go over that homework with the teacher to find places that they are struggling. This helps the teacher and the student identify problem areas. After the homework is corrected and new problems have been assigned for the students to do independently, the teacher will look at the new problems and give feedback. Once it is certain—from the perspective of both the teacher and the students—that the students have a good grip on the learning target, they will be allowed to retake the assessment. There is no grade given for the work habits here, but the retake is not allowed without good work habits. Students who do not wish to show up for extra teaching and to do the work required to show mastery of a learning target do not get to retake the assessment. In this scenario, work habits are evaluated, but not graded.

As you start to change your assessment practices, you may find it easier to count work habits as a part of the final grade. If so, make a category in your gradebook called Work Habits and list all these assignments in this category. Be careful not to weight this category more than 10% to 15% of the total grade. In this category you can list the homework assignments you want to record. You can consider whether or not a student completed the work, or you can track student preparedness in this manner. If tracking completion is something you, as a teacher, want to do in the gradebook, but you do not want to count the completion toward the calculated grade, make a work habits category worth 0%.

Leveling and accommodations

Leveling the assessments has two objectives. First, leveling is a way to organize an assessment. Each assessment would include questions in three different levels. Second, leveling is a way to distinguish the mastery level that a particular student has achieved according to the assessment the student chooses to take.

You might be saying to yourself right now, "I already put different level questions on my tests." We understand that, and we agree with you; however, let us explain further. Teachers can distinguish the level of questions on an assessment, and group them according to increasing level of difficulty. Each separate skill can be measured on an assessment that has three unique level questions. The teachers then can have their own procedures for deciding on a grade for the skill. Students who can do only Level 1 questions correctly might receive an overall grade for a skill that reflects initial mastery of the material. This initial mastery level can be any number you want in your gradebook. For simplicity's sake here, we will deal with initial mastery as a grade of 70. Students who can successfully complete Level 2 questions as well as Level 1 questions can be given a grade that reflects standard mastery over the skill being assessed. This grade can be 85 in the gradebook. Students who can successfully complete all three levels of questions can be given a grade that reflects advanced mastery over the material. This can be given as a 100 in the gradebook. It should be explained here that by "successfully completes," we do not necessarily mean 100% correct. If there are eight Level 1 questions on an assessment, and a student correctly answers seven of them and makes a minor error on the last one, this is still successful completion of the Level 1 question set. With the leveling of assessments, there is a lot of teacher discretion used. The key is to find a way that best works for you and to be consistent.

A discussion of leveling typically leads directly into a discussion of accommodations. Under this grading system, accommodations are easy to make since every student has them. Students are met where they are and graded on mastery of the new skill set at whatever level they can achieve. There are instances in which students can receive a top score for achieving initial mastery level of a skill. Students with IEPs are given the same opportunities as every other student in the class. If a student with an IEP wants to take an advanced mastery assessment because he feels like the current skill is something he really understands, he will be allowed to do so. His grading scale might simply change a little.

Another way students get accommodations is in the amount of aid they need to be successful. A student might try an initial mastery-level assessment and not be successful (for a grade of 70). This same student might still be unsuccessful on a second attempt, but if given a prompt or permission to use notes, can successfully complete the assessment. This (on a retake only), could be assigned a grade of 60 in the gradebook. Accommodations are handled in this grading system very easily. Sometimes creativity is required, but every student can be given necessary accommodations to help achieve the goal of some level of mastery over every skill assessed in the class.

Lifelines for teachers

Finally, as you set up your gradebook, here are some important items to note. Remembering these will provide valuable lifelines to help you to avoid sinking in frustration:

- All gradebook categories do not have to carry the same weight.
- Sometimes you may spend half of a grading period on an item and only two weeks on another. Every category does not have to have an equal number of assignments.
- Some skills are more important to your particular class.
- All assignments in the gradebook do not have to be out of 100 points. Make grades into averages as you proceed.

- You do not have to enter percentages into the gradebook if you determine the grades based on your knowledge of the student's mastery.
- You do not have to count every assignment or everything you mark.

Examples of grade reports are found at the end of this book.

What is on the horizon?

You have some ideas now about the ways in which you can assess student learning. You also know something about reporting that assessment in a gradebook. As you take the plunge into changing your gradebook, you may wonder what the ripple effects might be. In the next chapter, we consider the effects for students who find themselves at very different places in the academic journey.

7

Standards-Based Gradebook: Case Studies

First transition: Changing the gradebook and first reactions

We know that the teacher has mixed reactions to changing how the gradebook is set up. As students and parents experience these changes, their reactions may not be as amenable as one might anticipate. Let's look back at Jennifer, Tommy, and Andy and some typical first reactions from students, parents, and teachers.

Jennifer: Standards Based Report #1—Initial Report

Student: **Jennifer**
Class: **Pre-calculus**

Average: **85.00%**

Functions 40%		
Assignment	**Points Possible**	**Points Earned**
Exponential Functions	100	88
Quadratic Functions	100	82
Cubic Functions	100	
		Category Average:**95.00%**

Trigonometry 50%		
Assignment	**Points Possible**	**Points Earned**
Unit Circle	100	
Trig Ratios	100	
Trig Identities	100	
Inverses	100	
		Category Average: %

Series 10%		
Assignment	**Points Possible**	**Points Earned**
Explicit and Recursive	100	
Convergence	100	
Divergence	100	
Binomial Theorem	100	
		Category Average: %

JENNIFER: I cannot believe it. This teacher seems to only do tests. No homework grades! Thank you, thank you, thank you. The best part is I won't have to do any work to ace this class. I got this under control.

JENNIFER'S MOM: Jennifer said something to me about how her math class doesn't have homework anymore. Not sure I believe that, but as long as I don't get a call, I'll take her word for it.

Generally, the first reaction from students who have done historically well on tests is that they are completely in favor of standards-based grading. They hear "we don't grade you on homework or classwork," and they translate that into "I can continue not to do any work and be fine." In the beginning, this group will adore the change and even go so far as to boast about their lack of studying. If you ever have a group that will support the change, this is your group. And these students' parents will be behind it because the students will appear happy, something that many of them have not been regarding school for a long time.

JENNIFER'S TEACHER: This may be the first time that I can remember that Jennifer and I seem to be on the same page. She actually smiled when I talked about the changes as if she just made a new friend.

Tommy: Standards Based Report #1—Initial Report

Student: **Tommy**
Class: **Biology**

Average: **64.00%**

Cells 40%		
Assignment	**Points Possible**	**Points Earned**
Prokaryotic & Eukaryotic	100	68
4 Major Molecules	100	60
Chemical Reactions	100	
Growth & Reproduction	100	
	Category Average: **64.00%**	

Interdependence 30%		
Assignment	**Points Possible**	**Points Earned**
Interactions	100	
Population Data	100	
Biological Succession	100	
Changes on Environment	100	
	Category Average: **%**	

Heredity 30%		
Assignment	**Points Possible**	**Points Earned**
Genetics	100	5
Hybrid Crosses	100	9
Inheritance	100	8
Meiosis	100	8
Emerging Technologies	100	
	Category Average: **%**	

TOMMY: Seriously? I always do my work, come to class prepared, and now all of a sudden I get a 64 for busting my tail. A 64? I am going to fail. I am going to be grounded for life.

TOMMY'S DAD: This new grading system doesn't make any sense. What happened to homework, quizzes, and tests? I send my kid to school to get prepared for college and build a strong work ethic. All of a sudden, work ethic doesn't mean anything, and the school lets this teacher focus everything on one, two, or three tests. I even heard kids can retake tests till they make 100. My kid is getting punished.

Generally, the first reaction from students who have been strong workers is one of pure terror. Both they and their parents are trying to figure out how this system fits into their knowledge of school, which is work hard and turn in your assignments. The focus of Tommy and his dad are about completing work, not performance. Completion of work should override poor performance on assessments.

TOMMY'S TEACHER: This is hard. Tommy did everything I asked him to do and everything I assigned to the class prior to both of the first two assessments, yet he is failing. How do I explain to Tommy that doing the work is just not good enough? I am unsure if this is the right thing to do, but it is clear Tommy is already struggling with my cells unit. What should I do?

Andy: Standards Based Report #1—Initial Report

Student: **Andy**
Class: **English 10**

Average: **80.00%**

Language and Grammar 40%		
Assignment	**Points Possible**	**Points Earned**
Eight parts of speech	100	88
Usage	100	
Mechanics	100	
Sentence Structure	100	
	Category Average: **88.00%**	

Writing 30%		
Assignment	**Points Possible**	**Points Earned**
Modes, Audience, Purpose	100	50
Prewriting	100	80
Essay—Intro/Thesis	100	
Essay—Support	100	
Essay—Conclusion	100	
Revision	100	
	Category Average:**65.00%**	

Literature 30%		
Assignment	**Points Possible**	**Points Earned**
Romeo and Juliet Act 1	100	85
Romeo and Juliet Act 2	100	
Romeo and Juliet Act 3	100	
Speak—Asst 1	100	
Speak—Asst 2	100	
	Category Average: **85.00%**	

ANDY: I am not really sure what the big deal is with the change. We are still in school and the teacher is still teaching. 80. Yeah, that works, I'm fine.

ANDY'S MOM: Andy brought home his progress report, and he has an 80. That's about what we expect. Don't really know what all these items are that are written everywhere, but they look like English stuff to me. Man, I hated reading those English books, but Andy looks like he is doing well with it.

In Andy's case we have an example of a Language Arts (English) class in which he has grades throughout the categories. Andy and his mom don't necessarily care about the categories or the changes, but primarily are just concerned right now with the average. In all, it's not much different from before for either mom or Andy. The difference starts to take shape with the teacher.

ANDY'S TEACHER: Take a look at this progress report. Wow, it's clear as day to me. Andy needs some help on learning the ways different modes of writing can be used for specific purposes and audiences. I wonder what I can do to help him in that area. Right now I feel over my head trying to match what I am doing to the correct standards-based category. I really wonder how I can use this report to assist Andy and some of the other students who don't usually get my attention. Now that I have this information, I just need to figure out what to do with it. This is overwhelming and scary, but that's why I get paid the big bucks, right?

Second transition: Instruction and behavior impacting performance

After the initial setup and implementation of the gradebook changes, the second transition takes shape, and that is where the true value in the change begins to unfold. In this transition, the changes force the teacher and student into a situation where decisions about learning must happen. No longer is the student able to hide, and no longer can the teacher avoid expecting a higher level of performance from the students. This is where the power of the changes can transform conversations into clear expectations for learning as opposed to conversations stuck on behavior.

Jennifer: Standards Based Report #2—Later in the Term

Student: **Jennifer** Average: **INC**
Class: **Pre-calculus**

Functions 40%		
Assignment	**Points Possible**	**Points Earned**
Exponential Functions	100	88
Quadratic Functions	100	82
Cubic Functions	100	76
		Category Average:**82.00%**

Trigonometry 50%		
Assignment	**Points Possible**	**Points Earned**
Unit Circle	100	50*
Trig Ratios	100	60*
Trig Identities	100	75
Inverses	100	
		Category Average:*Inc

Series 10%		
Assignment	**Points Possible**	**Points Earned**
Explicit and Recursive	100	
Convergence	100	
Divergence	100	
Binomial Theorem	100	
		Category Average: **%**

Typically, with Jennifer, what may have started out as a seemingly good situation will eventually hit a point at which

Jennifer cannot achieve mastery without being prepared; therefore, her grades will suffer. So, in this situation, we made up this mock case which moved right into the next unit.

JENNIFER'S TEACHER: Jennifer was doing fine at the beginning of the term but now is really struggling. Not doing her homework has certainly caught up with her. I have decided to override her grade with an Incomplete until she is properly prepared to show proficiency in what we are doing. So, for the entire Trig unit in the places in which she is having some trouble, she will need to turn in all of her work to me, and that work must be done correctly. Once she does this and she meets with me to go over it for final questions, she can then come on her own time after school to retake the Unit Circle and Trig Ratios assessments. I told Jennifer failing is not an option. She wants a grade; therefore, she must show me she can perform.

JENNIFER: I cannot believe my teacher. I thought I could just take these tests and be fine. Now I have to do my work. My teacher will not let me take the remaining Trig tests until I work with her on the Unit Circle. In order to retake the Unit Circle, I also must complete all my homework for the Unit Circle correctly just to take the test again and bring up my 50. This was supposed to be easier!

JENNIFER'S MOM: Jennifer talked me into calling her math teacher to complain about her Incomplete. I didn't quite understand how she had an Incomplete when she had taken the tests, but then her teacher explained that it wasn't an option to fail and explained exactly where Jennifer needed to improve. It was a strange conversation—the teacher was not mad, upset, or defensive. And I laughed when I realized Jennifer could retake the tests and improve. She always tells me how much better she would do if she were just tested without all of this busywork. I guess Jennifer got what she wished for!

Tommy: Standards Based Report #2—Later in the Term

Student: **Tommy**
Class: **Biology**

Average: **72.00%**

Cells 40%		
Assignment	**Points Possible**	**Points Earned**
Prokaryotic & Eukaryotic	100	68
4 Major Molecules	100	60
Chemical Reactions	100	78
Growth & Reproduction	100	82
		Category Average: **72.00%**

Interdependence 30%		
Assignment	**Points Possible**	**Points Earned**
Interactions	100	
Population Data	100	
Biological Succession	100	
Changes on Environment	100	
		Category Average: **%**

Heredity 30%		
Assignment	**Points Possible**	**Points Earned**
Genetics	100	5
Hybrid Crosses	100	9
Inheritance	100	8
Meiosis	100	8
Emerging Technologies	100	
		Category Average: **%**

As Tommy moves farther into the term, he finds himself beginning to ask better questions with a focus on trying to get feedback from his teacher prior to taking the assessments. But what happens with his earlier grades? Is he reliant only on what he can do for future assessments?

TOMMY'S TEACHER: I began trying to provide some better feedback to Tommy and some of my other kids prior to our assessments. I noticed that this helped Tommy progress more quickly, as I know he is working hard but just didn't really know what or how to study for the assessments. He and his dad keep asking for extra credit. As the teacher, I know Tommy doesn't need extra credit. He just needs the opportunity to show me he has learned the content from his first two tests. So we struck a deal in which he could take an additional assessment on those two tests only after showing me he really knew the material. When he came by, I asked him a few questions to make sure he was really ready to retest.

TOMMY: I am beginning to feel a little better about class, but this is really hard. I actually have to know what my teacher is teaching. We did make a deal about how I could make up the tests I did badly on earlier. I wish there was extra credit, but I guess this is better than nothing.

TOMMY'S DAD: Tommy is really working hard lately on his Biology. I'll give him credit that he has not backed down. After talking with the teacher, I feel a lot better about the retest situation. I'm glad to know he will be able to bring his grade up. I was worried that he would have an F on his report card.

Andy: Standards Based Report #2—Later in the Term

Student: **Andy** Average: **83.00%**
Class: **English 10**

Language and Grammar 40%		
Assignment	**Points Possible**	**Points Earned**
Eight parts of speech	100	88
Usage	100	80
Mechanics	100	
Sentence Structure	100	
	Category Average: **84.00%**	
Writing 30%		
Assignment	**Points Possible**	**Points Earned**
Modes, Audience, Purpose	100	50
Prewriting	100	80
Essay—Intro/Thesis	100	86
Essay—Support	100	75
Essay—Conclusion	100	85
Revision	100	80
	Category Average:**76.00%**	
Literature 30%		
Assignment	**Points Possible**	**Points Earned**
Romeo and Juliet Act 1	100	85
Romeo and Juliet Act 2	100	Inc
Romeo and Juliet Act 3	100	95
Speak—Asst 1	100	
Speak—Asst 2	100	
	Category Average: **90.00%**	

As Andy moves through the term, he looks like he is doing fairly well across the board with one hiccup in the Modes, Audience, and Purpose assessment. However, Andy did not complete the assessment for the *Romeo and Juliet* Act 2. In this case, his teacher did not have any evidence to show what Andy did or did not know so the grade is an incomplete.

ANDY'S TEACHER: Andy missed the *Romeo and Juliet* Act 2 assessment, and he and I keep missing each other to get the assessment completed. I could give him a zero, but I feel confident that doesn't tell me anything about what he knows. Looking at his two other grades for *Romeo and Juliet*, I feel confident that he knows what is happening and understands the material at a high level. I am going to leave it as an Incomplete that does not affect his grade. I think that right now I have the information I need to make this determination. But I will also see how he does later when we move into the novel, *Speak*.

ANDY: My teacher told me that I was good to go for the *Romeo and Juliet* pieces. But my teacher also let me know that what happens when we read and are assessed on that book *Speak* will play into how my teacher ultimately decides on that incomplete piece. If I keep up those high grades in literature, I am good on the literature piece. But if my grade goes down in literature, I may have to get that assessment done. No problem, I'll keep them up.

ANDY'S MOM: A couple weeks back, Andy was sick for about five days. I was worried that would really mess him up, but his teacher let me know that we'll just keep moving forward. The teacher let me know that Andy was doing well in literature, so as long as he continues to do well, Andy's grade will be a good shape. Sounds like a teacher with some common sense.

Third transition: Continuous improvement

In this final stage, we will not be analyzing a progress report for Jennifer, Tommy, and Andy. Instead, we will emphasize that in this phase, the teachers are continually tweaking what information they use from the progress report to help better instruct the student and impact student learning. In the third transition, the teacher uses the data in the gradebook to make informed instructional decisions. The teacher no longer has to guess the areas in which a student needs to improve; the focus of the improvement is on learning goals.

The third transition creates the change in conversation for Jennifer, Tommy and Andy as follows:

On the traditional progress report, Jennifer appeared lazy and difficult. In the third transition, Jennifer knows specifically what she needs to learn, at what level, and what specific actions are required for her to reach that level. She does what she needs to do and she, her mom, and the teacher all know and can all agree what that is.

JENNIFER: I finally get it. This teacher wants me to do well and knows when I need to do work and when I don't. I wish all my teachers could get this. School is much better when you don't have to do a bunch of meaningless assignments.

On the traditional progress report, Tommy, a hard worker and a good kid, appeared to be succeeding. In the third transition, Tommy's teacher is better equipped to help him focus his hard work. This focus allows Tommy to learn material at his own pace. His efforts translate into meaningful learning as opposed to ritual workload compliance.

TOMMY: This change was really hard for me. I mean, we spend years learning that working hard is the only thing that matters. I am glad that what I work on now is actually supposed to help me get better. Knowing that my teacher is focused on whether I understand, not when I understand, takes a lot of pressure off of me. I know my teacher will give me opportunities to improve my grade, and when I get the higher grade, I feel like I really know what I am doing.

On the traditional progress report, Andy's needs appear to be met. In the third transition, Andy becomes actively involved in the learning process, no longer happy just blending in. He is part of making decisions about his learning and, even more importantly, he can distinguish what he does well.

ANDY: It's pretty neat to know that I am good at different things in my classes. I always thought that I was average in everything. Now I can see where I do things well. Also, my teacher seems to know me better and really wants to help me do well. It's really nice to get back stuff from my teacher, and when I need to do something better, be able to concentrate on something that is specific. It makes doing better seem less overwhelming.

■

Recognizing the impact on students caused by a standards-based progress report is a process that takes time. Students perceive that impact individually along the way. Parents normally fall in line with their children; that is, when their child is happy and performing well, so are the parents. As for the teachers, the impact of the third transition is the most powerful. Teachers become educators focused on improvement in which they are continually tweaking:

- The targets listed in the gradebook
- Intervention strategies and ideas
- Assessments to determine student grades
- Instructional practices to improve grades from the start
- The level of acceptable proficiency
- The number of grades.

What is so nice about the above list? That is what teaching means: tweaking what we, as educators, do to impact student learning positively. Changing assessment practices is the gateway to this positive impact.

8

Personal Perspectives

Lisa Beard
Science Teacher

THE PAST FOUR years have taught me that assessment should not measure the route someone takes to get to a certain destination, but rather, it should reflect whether or not the destination was reached. I have come to realize that homework, class work, quizzes, and laboratories are just means to reach a given destination, such as achieving a particular learning target in a chemistry class. Initially, I was conflicted about the degree that each one of these routes contributes in the assessment of my students. I faced challenges to my own pedagogy and educational philosophies. What emerged from this change was a student-driven atmosphere. The funny part is, after all that effort and fret, it wasn't that hard. All I had to do was simply teach. Not teach the old way, but in an empowering way that is standards-driven.

Before I began teaching using the mastery approach, I relied primarily on lecture, demonstrations, and laboratory to teach chemical concepts. I was the captain and the students were my crew. Their job was to listen and learn as I performed amazing, mind-boggling experiments and thought-provoking, theory-oriented lectures. Laboratory experiments were conducted by my crew of students almost weekly, and I thought that as captain of this ship, I was doing an incredible job at teaching students how to explore the world. Little did I realize that while my students were busy manning the deck, more than half of them had no idea of how to read a compass or navigate a ship, let alone swim. Walk into my classroom on any given day, and the appearance was that the students were busy learning; however, in retrospect, some were only scrubbing the deck. The revelation of how much my students did not know came to me when I decided to assess only final work (such as tests), which meant that students were graded solely based on whether or not they had achieved the objectives. For the first time, I felt exposed. I realized the true effect of all the chemical rhetoric and theory used in class and knew that I would have to develop ways of fixing it before this ship sank.

Initially, I had many struggles. The most immediate was student apathy. I should have expected this, because the traditional system of grading is a completion-based system. If you do not count homework grades in your gradebook, it can become a problem to get students motivated to do their work. Let me be clear: Homework is a valuable and necessary component in a student's mastery of objectives. It cannot be ignored. I tried many scenarios hoping to lead students to take charge of their learning, but I found that I was stretching myself to the limit in order to get them there.

It took a drastic, yet simple measure to make it a reality. I gave a simple mandate: "You are not allowed to test until all homework is complete." As you can imagine, I had several who did not take the next test. The consequence put in place was mandatory lunches with me until all work was complete and the missed test was taken. In addition, for those students, the score recorded in the gradebook was an Incomplete until they completed the necessary steps to take the summative assessment over the given objectives. (The Incomplete seemed to reflect urgency on the student's part to "kick it in high gear" and get on task with the learning the objectives.) Once the test was taken, they had to complete a self-assessment of the test, which evaluates their progress over the objectives. At that point, their Incomplete was replaced with their actual test score. This seemed to work well, but then I decided I wanted to try to help prevent as many students as possible from reaching that point. So, I implemented a new policy: "Every time you miss a homework assignment, your parents will be notified." For me, these two policies were a key in solving the apathy problems.

A second obstacle was student retention of the learning objectives. I found that by offering multiple opportunities to retest over concepts not mastered, students were less likely to retain what they learned or be able to apply it in a new setting. Those students who achieved the objectives without retest, however, were more likely to succeed at remembering the objectives. I had a hard time understanding how this could be true, until one day I had to take my children to one of their friends' house. I printed the directions from Google Maps, read those directions, loaded the kids in the car, and took off. Once I got onto unfamiliar roads, I found myself asking my children to read each direction to me. I simply could not remember turn by turn what I was supposed to do to reach my destination. I had to revisit my map.

I thought about how I give "maps" (stated learning objectives) to my students at the beginning of each class and each unit, but I never have the students monitor where they are, what journey they are on, or what turn they need to be making, as we are progressing through a unit. I only had them look again at the objectives as "I Can" statements a day or so prior to testing. The problem, I realized, was not necessarily in the frequency of the offering of retests, but in the lack of frequency over the self-evaluation of the objectives prior to testing. I knew students needed to revisit their "maps" more often during the process of learning in order for them to retain the information. Feedback in the form of homework, labs, and quizzes are all a part of this process. In the past, I considered the grades students made on this formative work as their feedback. After all, it is common sense that if students fail a quiz, they need to study that portion of the objectives before testing. Why do I need to bring it to their attention?

However, what I have found is that some students need the prodding to get them back on route. So, what I did additionally was have students track and evaluate their formative assessments to determine if they were on the right course. This process involved a written reflection after each assignment, a written summary of each learning objective, and peer teaching as needed. Thus, at each turn (each learning objective) students were more likely to remember the way to their destination. The students needing to retest decreased significantly and retention of material increased. For those who needed to retest, I assigned additional practice problems as well as mandatory tutoring time prior to retesting. This continual prodding along the way—getting students to focus on their maps, letting them see their route and their destination—was a success.

A third struggle was teacher overload. Yes, I did have to write several versions of homework practice and several versions of each test. I quickly became bogged down while grading different versions of tests and homework at various times throughout the grading period. Tracking progress was time-consuming. I became overwhelmed with the number of students who needed help at lunch and who wanted to retest over an objective. I came to realize that when the teacher is working harder than the student, something is wrong. That is the point that this whole process became easy. I gradually gave the students more responsibility for tracking their learning. As I did so, they became more independent as learners. Students became empowered as they took charge of each "turn-by-turn" direction. All I had to do was relinquish a little power and give the students more control.

Once I was able to turn tracking of objectives over to the student, I freed myself up to do what I do best—teach. I still perform amazing, mind-boggling experiments and give thought-provoking, theory-oriented lectures; however, it is now truly standards-driven. Because the students continually evaluate their own strengths and weaknesses, they know exactly when to pull into a port for supplies and when to speed ahead. When they do need additional help, tools have been set in place to help them change whatever setbacks that they experience along the way. Learning centers, manipulatives, computer programs, peer tutoring, and lunch remedials are a few of the tools put in place. And, when I see that they are failing to get themselves back on course, I just pull out their maps (their self-assessment binders) to see where they are.

Some of my greatest moments through this process occur when students who struggled through my class come to me the next year asking me to give them a stoichiometry problem (or some other chemistry problem) to solve on the white board or when a former student steps in during lunch just to help a currently struggling student. Having students return after their first year of college bragging about how easy freshman Chemistry was gives further confirmation that I am on trhe right track in my assessment practices. When a student cries or wants to give me a high five when she achieves an objective after working so hard to reach it, I have a feeling of sweet success. This process is an empowering exploration—for me and for the student!

■

Glenda Sullivan
English Teacher

I HAD TAUGHT twenty-six years in another system before transferring to Fairview High School. I wanted to try new experiences and to test new ideas rather than to float along till retirement. I knew that the way I had been doing things wasn't reaching everyone, but I had been taught in this manner and had made it just fine. I really didn't think the assessment process was the problem. I had always given certain tests on which students had to show high levels of proficiency in order to receive a passing grade, but I didn't (perhaps couldn't?) assess every skill adequately.

Changing the way I assess student learning, record grades, reteach material, and communicate with students has not been easy. Change really doesn't frighten me much, but I do worry about staying afloat because I tend to take on lots of responsibilities, and I want to do everything to the best of my ability. I was also worried that the change might negatively affect student behaviors and grades and perhaps harm my class enrollment. Perhaps students would avoid the upper-level courses I teach if they were faced with lower grades.

Thanks to a bit of coaching from fellow teachers and administrators, I quickly became convinced that changing my assessment procedures was the lifeline my students needed to help them perform better both now and in the future in college. I started cautiously, and before long ran into an obstacle.

Teaching English differs from teaching most other subjects. It involves addressing many targets simultaneously—literature, writing, language, research, communication, informational text, media, and logic—which represent the eight standards in Tennessee's state curriculum. Under each of these eight are many learning objectives. Singling out each objective can be difficult, and isolating them isn't always the best way to address student needs. I realized right away that I was in over my head.

Any given English test covered at least three or four standards and a dozen or more learning objectives. Students who had previously made good grades were not doing so. I soon found myself drowning in a sea of test papers and conferences. I described my dilemma to the department head, other teachers, the assistant principals, and to the principal. Then, I started talking to former students, teachers at other schools, my husband (also an English teacher), random strangers at education-related events, and the heavens. At first, only the English teachers could visualize the problems involved, but eventually everyone saw that English was hard to assess by specific, individual targets.

After a department meeting revealed that none of us was completely thrilled with our progress, the principal arranged for us to meet with a representative from the state Department of Education. At that session, we realized that we needed to vertically align some repetitive targets and agreed that we could teach a number of topics at the same time with several targets appearing on the same assessment, without necessarily having separate grades for each. Later, my principal, my department chair, and I spoke via conference call with a language arts teacher in another state to get some ideas. The conference call led us to further consider combining and reducing targets as well.

Finally, some of the teachers in the English department

conducted an eye-opening visit to a middle school that was utilizing a similar approach to assessment. The teachers there were assessing a limited number of targets, not by design, but just because instruction was working in that way. Seeing their work confirmed our decision to align the targets vertically so that each teacher was responsible for covering fewer targets annually, while determining how to streamline the targets to make them manageable and reachable.

These same teachers spent an entire day making certain that related skills were covered in an appropriate sequence by examining all the targets. It was a difficult process, and there were some targets that had to be taught in all four levels although nuanced specifically to the grade level's curriculum. Most skills could be divided based on a particular state assessment for that grade level.

This new alignment was introduced in our next departmental meeting where it garnered much appreciation. Everyone was glad for a more manageable list, and most of this work made immediate sense to everyone without any need for clarification.

As I began making my way toward the end-of-course tests, AP exams, and state writing assessments again, I saw, with great satisfaction, that this assessment style was working. Students really needed to master the targets to do well on tests. Since I was new to this assessment procedure, I made some mistakes. I tried to make sure my students didn't suffer from my mistakes; they were allowed to retest, to come in for further study, to do extra work to prepare for retesting, and to help me to become a better teacher. Students were encouraged to evaluate their progress and my instruction and to offer suggestions and comments. There was no extra credit, but no one seemed to mind. On each test I included some of the previous targets to make certain that students weren't just storing information in their short-term memory, passing the test, and then dumping the information. By the end of the year, my students performed well on our state's English II End-of-Course tests, the Tennessee Writing Assessment, and in-class assessments. My current students' performance on the Advanced Placement exams improved when compared to the previous year's class. Students reported improved ACT scores (if they had previously taken the ACT) and most seemed satisfied that no one was out to hurt them or their grades. Rather, we started to have some better conversations about what was going on in class.

Students no longer asked, "Why am I not making an A, B, C, etc., in this class?" and, instead, posed questions such as, "What do I need to do to learn this target?" When I talked to parents about student progress, I could point out specific areas of mastery, partial mastery, and non-mastery on the progress report. We could talk about how targets related to each other and what they meant to becoming a better communicator, writer, and student. Students could no longer hide the fact that they just didn't get some target by doing well on all the other ones. They could no longer avoid targets by just choosing to avoid the work and taking a zero. The students' understanding of what they were trying to achieve was greater. It was a relief not to hear, "Why are we doing this?"

Where did problems with this assessment procedure arise? Sometimes the problem was the students' need for more formative assessments. I did have at least one formative for every summative, but when it looked as if everyone was on top of the requirement, I would schedule the summative. Sometimes I was wrong because the students were not ready. Another problem was the need for more time. We needed more time to conference individually; sometimes I needed more time to re-evaluate a student's mastery. Occasionally, I would find myself slipping back into old habits. It was a work-in-progress.

Sometimes I find that a specific target relates to one piece of literature differently than it does to another. Certain types of literary elements, such as irony, are more prominent in one author's work than in another. Also, the teaching of writing changes depending on the mode of writing being discussed.

A big source of concern among the department was how

to record progress. Sometimes teachers found it more effective to record mastery by units covered. I could never make this work for me. Again, I wanted the record to make sense to everyone who saw it. What are the targets? How is the student doing? Where are the successes? Where do we need to work? For example, I couldn't provide that clarity in something labeled Poetry Unit Scores. I tried, but I could not make the record as meaningful or as helpful.

Assessing in this way seems to be getting easier now. Sure, every now and then there are problems, but I never find myself wanting to give up. For me, part of the joy of teaching is finding out what works, and what doesn't, and what adjustments to make. I really wouldn't want my child, or any other, to be taught by teachers who weren't always improving and making those discoveries.

■

Jennifer Anton
Math Teacher

AS I BEGIN to reflect on how standards-based assessment and grading has worked for me, I feel the need to back up and discuss where I started. I had been teaching eight years when my family moved, and I began teaching in a new state, district, and school. During this first year, I was invited to begin implementing a new grading style in my classes for the final grading period. I am always up for new challenges, and so I graciously accepted the invitation. A few weeks into my initial plunge I was frustrated, but since I had given my word, I maintained the course. At the end of the school year, I picked the brains of several teachers and administrators at the school to help me make changes I could implement without destroying the purpose behind the change. Based on the feedback I received, along with some of my own trial and error, I now make changes to my system annually. These changes are part of my growth as a teacher, and I am certain that I will continue to morph my assessment and grading system every year to meet my needs, the needs of the particular course I teach, and the needs of my students.

Implementation of this new system brought about many changes for me. The first change that must be mentioned is that grades went down. This was shocking to me, so I wanted to mention it so that you are not alarmed if it happens to you. I think that the main reason for grades initially going down is that students needed to adjust to having grades that required evidence of true learning as opposed to grades that are fluffed with grades for attendance, preparedness, effort, participation, or any other task that is not academically relevant. The change in gradebook did, however, help me focus remediation for students on weaknesses as they occurred in the gradebook, and that remedied much of the initial dive in the student grades.

The second change is that I become a master of multitasking. I now like to use the term organized chaos to refer to my classroom during differentiated instruction times as well as during reteaching and testing. I have always thought of myself as a multitasker, but my first attempt at changing my assessment and grading practices took multitasking to a whole new level. I found myself carrying on several different conversations at one time while looking at another student's evidence of mastery. Then there were times when these events were occurring while another teacher or administrator would enter. This was very cumbersome for me in the beginning, and there were many days that I felt as if I were in the center of a hurricane. But, after I put into place some concrete logistical rules regarding reteaching and retesting, the process became comfortably manageable.

The third change for me was that I had to gain confidence in instructional areas in which I was previously uncomfortable. These included changing lessons daily as student needs dictated I change them, collaborating with other teachers and truly listening to what my colleagues had to offer, and being creative with handling student behaviors that were inappropriate without using the grade to punish the behavior. All of these issues required a paradigm shift for me and inherently made my classroom culture change. The change in culture was most evident when the students realized that poor behavior did not get them out of the academic requirements. Regardless of the misbehavior, the goal of the class was proficiency of learning targets. The students quickly made the connection that misbehaving only meant a delay in the work that had to be done. Misbehavior made the situation worse for the student, and no longer did misbehavior cause a student to receive a zero for work related to a concept the student found difficult.

The elimination of this coping mechanism truly changed my classroom, and, at this point, I was a believer in the system. At the end of this first grading period, a student who, under the previous grading system was routinely a behavior problem, received his grades. He said, "Mrs. Anton, you have to be kidding me, I have a B?" I said, "Yes, you have a B; you have done well."

His reply was, "But I thought you hated me." This conversation gives me pause even today. I have never given students grades based on how I felt about them, but it makes me wonder how many of my former students thought I might have. I knew, on this day, that while I did not have the system right, I was willing to put forth any necessary effort to make the new grading system work for me.

When I think of how assessment and grading occurred in my classroom before and after the changes described, the difference looks something like this box:

> A look at before and after assessment and grading changes were made:
>
> **Before:** Johnny, if you will please blindly copy Susie's homework and tests (for your test corrections) on material you clearly do not understand, then maybe the grading fairy will sprinkle magic grading fairy dust, and you will get your B.
>
> **After:** Johnny, you are having a great deal of trouble with solving quadratics. Here are some concrete ideas so you can improve at it. I guarantee your grade will change to reflect your understanding when you master the material.

I never realized, or maybe never thought about, how little the way I was reporting grades reflected the individual student mastery of material. I taught, I gave homework, I gave quizzes, projects, and tests. I graded them all, recorded most of them, and spent a lot of time at the end of grading periods trying to figure out a way to improve my students' grades so that the grade would reflect what I knew the student had mastered. Changing my assessment and grading practices was a revelation for me. I had finally found a way for the grade to reflect what the student knew, without having to circumvent the system to make it happen. The couple of weeks leading up to the end of a grading period are stressful. The sheer number of students rushing to retest grows and becomes very hectic, but I am thankful that this rush occurs to show mastery of material. This is a drastic improvement over the rush to try to make me invent some sort of meaningless extra-credit assignment so that students can improve their grades. I would always rather answer a student who asks, "How can I show mastery over a specific learning target?" than answer "What can I do to be able to pass?"

■

Todd Stinson
Former Math Teacher and Current Assistant Principal

IT WAS DIFFICULT to begin the process of drastically changing the way I graded. I can remember vividly having to explain our rationale many times to a variety of people—students, parents, as well as fellow teachers. There were times that the transition became so frustrating that I questioned the motives and the probability of success myself. Slowly, however, most of my students came around to the idea of mastering skills and concepts. By about the fourth or fifth week, students who were satisfied with an 80% average during the previous grading period were coming to me on their own time asking me how to move to the highest level of mastery. It was surprising to me. I had tried to push and prod these students to achieve more and had been met with apathy. In a relatively short period of time, they had become intrinsically motivated to succeed.

I don't want to be misleading. Not every kid was suddenly transformed into a model student. There were some to whom just getting by was still good enough. But I found two things to be the case:

1.) The number of students desiring to show mastery of material had drastically increased.

2.) Across the board and with very few exceptions, the grade applied at the end of the grading cycle was a much better reflection of what my students could and could not do.

Just as I was getting used to grading for mastery, I made another transition—from teacher to assistant principal. This new position brought a new perspective. I began to see (and continue to see) different kinds of struggles and successes. I moved from being a colleague and co-teacher to suddenly being asked for help in answering a variety of questions. I was now expected to be an expert in assessment even though I knew I did not have all the answers. At first I was very frustrated and thought to myself, "Just do it. Quit asking questions and making excuses! Make it work for you." I avoided as many of these conversations as I could because they made me uncomfortable. But I did my best to learn and grow, just as the teachers did, and eventually began to enjoy talking about assessment with teachers. It was a topic that I truly believed had a huge impact on our students. I also served as a buffer between Mr. Donen and teachers. As you might imagine, there was more than a little frustration for teachers who were trying something this unusual; however, the most enjoyable role I took on was as a sounding board for teachers ready to tackle the challenge. It was exciting to hear how an initially hesitant teacher had grown to the point that he or she was on the leading edge of this change.

At this point in our journey, most of the teachers have bought into the idea of assessment and grading based on mastery and proficiency. With few exceptions, the difficulties are not a result of philosophical differences; rather they stem from a misunderstanding of what I consider to be minor details of a system such as this. For instance, one of the basic principles of our grading is that we do not use homework to inflate (or deflate) a student's grade. A few of our teachers have taken that to mean that they must grade everything that they assign. They agree that completion grades serve to distort the accuracy and, therefore, grade *every* assignment for accuracy and record those in the gradebook. This creates a lot of unnecessary work for the teacher and fails to provide accurate information. In turn, these teachers become discouraged with the system and tend to want to go back to their former methods.

One of the most frustrating things for me is to encounter teachers who allow external issues to interfere with carrying out their primary goal of teaching kids. Some teachers are still convinced that the best way to get students to behave properly is by negatively adjusting their grade for misbehaviors ranging from talking in class, to not bringing materials, to not completing homework. Although this may be effective for a short period of time, it completely distorts the meaning of the student's grade. I have participated in numerous conversations centering on "teaching responsibility" that began with the phrase "when they get to college. . ." In these cases, I have tried to refocus the conversation on what teachers are trying to accomplish with their grading. I encourage teachers to reflect on the purpose and the meaning of the grades that they allocate a student. The bottom line should be that the grades we give students should be accurate reflections of what they can and cannot do.

Some very rewarding and inspiring stories have arisen as we made this change as well. I have seen a dramatic drop in office referrals. In the past, when a student bombed a test, there was little or no chance for passing the class. When faced with this dilemma, students acted up, treated the teacher with disdain or disrespect, and were willing to do anything not to be in class. All of that changes when you allow students to prove what they can do all the way to the end. Students and teachers become less adversarial in a system like this, and correction becomes less personal without being impersonal.

As I began having conversations with students who were struggling academically, I noticed that the content of these discussions changed. I saw the students taking more ownership in their academic success. I was surprised to hear teenagers who were able to convey what they needed to do to improve their grades in terms of standards. This is an encouraging transformation. Conversations with parents have changed as well. Now when a parent calls to complain about a grade in a class, I can direct them to the standards and encourage them to send their child to the teacher for extra help, confident that the teacher can help and will be focused on helping the student understand the material better. For these teachers, the gradebook is no longer about behaviors in class, it is about what the student can and cannot do.

■

Tony Donen
Principal

"A SCHOOL ADMINISTRATOR is an educational leader who promotes the success of all students by advocating, nurturing, and sustaining a school culture and instructional program conducive to student learning and staff professional growth," according to the Interstate

School Leaders Licensure Consortium. The Tennessee Instructional Leadership Standards describe an effective educational leader as one who "implements a systematic, coherent approach to bring about the continuous growth in the academic achievement of all students."

When I began the process of analyzing assessment, it quickly became apparent that the communication of assessments was integral in the success of learning. It also became apparent that the most obvious place of our communication was in our traditional gradebook. I had no real idea at the beginning of this process just how flawed the traditional gradebook was until we started to make changes. This transformation process has, at times, seemed overwhelming and impossible. Yet, there is no doubt that how we have been grading and assessing kids for years is not sound and often misleading. We have continued to accept it simply because that is the way we were graded and assessed, and we turned out okay. The only problem I have is that *okay* is not good enough. Our goal is to help kids learn, and if we are communicating about everything else except learning through our grading and assessment practices, we are consistently contradicting ourselves in what our main goal is in education—student learning.

In the state of Tennessee, every high school student, regardless of socio-economic background, learning disability, or post-high school plans, is required to take the ACT. This requirement in Tennessee is relatively new, but if you look elsewhere around the country, numerous states started this requirement four and five years ago. In addition, at this point in American education and accountability, states have also begun to work together, as demonstrated by the American Diploma Project, to develop a set standard of achievement and accountability across the nation regardless of urban, rural, or suburban setting. Performance is the criterion for success. Grading and assessment practices are more important now than ever before, and we cannot continue to use a process that is ambiguous and ineffective in communicating student strengths and areas to improve. We must find a way to communicate deliberately, succinctly, and properly so everyone knows how to close the gap between where a student is and where the student needs to be in order to learn. As the TILS Standard B advocates, it is the administrator's responsibility to create "a school culture and climate based on high expectations conducive to the success of all students."

The ideas presented in this book are only the beginning steps in the process of moving toward this end. We are just at the tip of the iceberg, as the next crucial and important steps in the process are engaging students in their own assessments and reflections and defining attainable plans of action.

Learning the skill of self-assessment provides students with the tools to identify their own strengths and weaknesses. The result is a more mature, intrinsically motivated individual. That is the definition of a life-long learner. If a student cannot self-assess and determine how to define a personal plan of action to address specific learning goals, we as educators have failed the student.

As I reflect on our journey, I note that our traditional gradebooks and assessment practices never addressed these plans in terms of content learning, because it was simply impossible to do so using the traditional gradebook. However, it became possible when we began this transition. All of our conversations then focused on learning. And when that happened, students were not afraid to formulate questions about the learning objectives, and they were more attentive to the direction given by the teacher in determining what to study and how to use their time effectively. Students began evolving into life-long learners.

During this process, I made several mistakes. I rushed teachers into making a change, and that caused resentment and resistance from some. I should have spent more time explaining, demonstrating, and providing an understanding of how our traditional grading and assessment practices were actually hurting kids. When it came to student testing, I began by thinking that it did not matter how many times a student had to retest; the issue was only *if* the student could learn it, and not when. But, even though I fully believe in this in theory, the practicality of the situation is that teachers simply run out of time and cannot manage endless retesting. What teachers are able to do, instead, is focus on better formative assessments and working out ways to help students on the front end.

Changing grading and assessment practices is not easy, nor is there a simple way to make the transition. The original ten teachers were not hesitant to express their likes or dislikes or worries about these practices, and they helped to stretch my thought process. I am thankful to teachers who were willing to share with me areas of concern to make the change better for both our students and our staff. Change involves time, working through the process, and knowing that what you can help create is a far better process, but not necessarily one that is completely fixed. Time is always the largest variable, and there is not enough time to make a perfect process. We had a broken system before we made the changes, and now have a less-broken, more student-friendly, and meaningful system. In the perfect world, we would have a process where each and every student could verbalize his or her own understandings and lack of understandings, and create a plan to close the gap. This is where we will strive, as this is where the most powerful learning will take place.

For our school, the process of moving toward a gradebook that was standards-based and focusing on better assessment practices has created a cultural change in how we do school. No longer do students just want to give up and think that they cannot meet the mark. Because more and more of the feedback is targeted to particular items, students are able to better manage what it is they need to do in order to make the grade they want. I used to hear consistently from students, whether it was Honors Pre-calculus class or freshmen English, "I just can't do it." And the answer was usually, "You need to try harder." Now, it's about identifying the exact piece or pieces of learning with which the student is struggling, and then providing opportunity and instruction to help the student in that struggle. Don't let me mislead you, however. This does create a problem. Students do spend more time with the teachers asking to be reassessed in areas where they were weak and non-proficient. As the principal of the school, I believe this is exactly where we need to focus our efforts in order to be the learning organization we hope to be.

Would I go through this process again as a principal knowing what I have learned and the struggles we have faced? Absolutely. When we started this process, grades went down. Every one of our teachers who began the process had at least one, if not more, problems that made the teacher question the change. Most teachers had thoughts of giving up. Once we moved through the initial phases and overcame obstacles, we all knew the changes were what we needed to do for kids. As each teacher became increasingly comfortable with a workable process for his or her classroom, all came to understand that going back to traditional grading and assessment practices is not an option. The only option is to keep working on improving our practices so that each child can meet and exceed our expectations as students, parents, teachers, and society.

My personal interest in improving our practices relates to my own family. My daughter is starting kindergarten this fall. It is my hope that the feedback given to her for her K–12 education is meaningful and sensible. She will become a life-long learner if she is able to self-assess her own strengths and weaknesses and can plan to build a system around herself to be successful. If she is unable to practice and learn this process because she never experiences nor is taught how to use targeted feedback, that is because we have lost the spirit of education. We are just grading and assessing primarily good behavior and conformity. Learning becomes secondary, and we end up perpetuating the cycle of education where students are unable to perform at high levels.

A life-long learner has learned how to learn. How we grade can launch our students on this perpetual voyage.

■

From All of Us EDUCATION CONSULTANT Rick Wormeli wrote in an article in the *National Association of Secondary School Principals*:

> What goes unlearned and unachieved because I decided to play it safe and not rock the boat? Students get one year to complete their current grade level, so it better be the best experience it can be. If educators mire students in ineffective practices that are justified only by teachers' comfort with the familiar, they sacrifice a significant amount of student growth. It is no longer acceptable for everyone to agree to let teachers differentiate and grade in their own ways if they are not proven effective; there are identified principles that work better than others.

We challenge you to make changes in your grading and assessment practices because it is the right thing to do with regards to the students, your course, and education.

Standards-based assessment and grading does not look the same for every teacher or every school, but the basic guiding principles are consistent. As you begin to make your changes, be able to answer the following questions:

- Are my student grades absent of bias, emotion, and fluff?

- Do I have evidence of mastery or non-mastery for each learning target?
- Do the grades of my students reflect a level of mastery that is the same as my evidence?
- Did I run my classroom in such a way that students were free to learn and given every opportunity to do so in the manner that fit *them* best?

These questions will keep your grades on course with the standards-based guidelines outlined in this book even when you change your method of implementation as you improve it every year.

As you go through the process for yourself, keep in mind that if you feel that you are overwhelmed, it is because you are. The feeling is a natural subconscious response telling you to ask for help. Do not be afraid to research, ask colleagues, and email other teachers to get ideas. There is no guarantee that any other teacher's ideas will work for you, but with enough examples and suggestions, you will be able to put together a masterpiece.

Resources and References

Books that Shaped Fairview High School's Assessment and Grading Practices

Arter, J. A., & Chappuis, J. (2006). *Creating & recognizing quality rubrics.* Portland, OR: Educational Testing Service.

Chappuis, J. (2009). *Seven strategies of assessment for learning.* Portland, OR: Educational Testing Service.

Chappuis, S., Stiggins, R. J., Arter, J. A., & Chappuis, J. (2006). *Assessment for learning: An action guide for school leaders.* Portland, OR: Educational Testing Service.

Davies, A. (2000). *Making classroom assessment work.* Courtenay, British Columbia: Classroom Connections International.

Davies, A., & Busick, K. (Eds.). (2007). *Classroom assessment: What's working in high schools?* Courtenay, British Columbia: Building Connections Publishing.

Gregory, K., Cameron, C., & Davies, A. (1997). *Setting and using criteria.* Courtenay, British Columbia: Connections Publishing.

Guskey, T. R., & Bailey, J. M. (2000). *Developing grading and reporting systems for student learning.* Thousand Oaks, CA: Corwin Press.

Guskey, T. R., & Schultz, T. (1996). *Implementing mastery learning.* Belmont, CA: Wadsworth Publishing.

Hills, J. R. (1990). *Measuring and evaluation in the classroom.* Columbus, OH: Charles Merrill Publishing Company.

Marzano, R. J. (2000). *Transforming classroom grading.* Alexandria, VA: Association for Supervision and Curriculum Development.

Marzano, R.J. (2006). *Classroom assessment and grading that works.* Alexandria, VA: Association for Supervision and Curriculum Development.

O'Connor, K. (2007). *A repair kit for grading: 15 fixes for broken grades.* Portland, OR: Educational Testing Service.

Reeves, D. (Ed.). (2007). *Ahead of the curve: The power of assessment to transform teaching and learning*. Bloomington, IA: Solution Tree.

Stiggins, R. J., Arter, J. A., Chappuis, J., & Chappuis, S. (2006). *Classroom assessment for student learning: Doing it right – using it well.* Portland, OR: Educational Testing Service.

Tomlinson, C.A., & Allan, S.D. (2000). *Leadership for differentiating schools & classrooms.* Alexandria, VA: Association for Supervision and Curriculum Development.

References (cited in book)

Arter, J. (2008, December). *Converting rubric scores to grades.* Handouts from session presented at the Educational Testing Service Conference on Sound Grading Practices: Linking Quality Assessment and Grading (pp. 10-19). Portland, OR.

Guskey, T. R. (1994). Making the grade: What benefits students. *Educational Leadership*, 52(2), 14-20.

Guskey, T. R. (2005). Zero Alternatives. *Principal Leadership*, 5(2), 49-53.

Hills, J. R. (1990). *Measuring and evaluation in the classroom*. Columbus, OH: Charles Merrill Publishing Company.

Marzano, R.J. (2006). *Classroom assessment and grading that works.* Alexandria, VA: Association for Supervision and Curriculum Development.

O'Connor, K. (2007). *A repair kit for grading: 15 fixes for broken grades.* Portland, OR: Educational Testing Service.

Glossary

Assessment	A measurement of a student's ability to perform a certain skill or achieve a given objective.
Essential outcomes/ Essential concepts/ Learning Essentials	A broad overview of each unit theme as defined by the state objectives as essential knowledge. In our school, these terms later became known as learning targets.
Formative assessment	Assessments that help the student work toward understanding the learning target. Formative assessments may include homework, classwork, and quizzes.
Gradebook	A physical record of a student's progress toward achieving a learning target. Gradebooks can be a written record or an electronic record.
Grade Compliance	Completion of work as opposed to mastery of material.
Learning objectives	Specific objectives defined by the learning target that are to be achieved by the student.
Learning targets	Specific goals as defined by the state for a given content area.

Leveling	Organizing assessments based upon mastery level the student has worked toward achieving.
Mastery level	The degree (level) at which a student reaches the learning target. Mastery levels may include non-mastery, initial mastery, mastery, and advanced mastery.
Self- assessment	An evaluation completed by the student of the mastery level of his/her progress toward learning the objectives of the class.
Summative assessment	An evaluation of a student's ability to achieve a learning objective. Summative assessments are given after several formative assessments over the same learning target. Examples of summative assessments include tests, projects, and reports.
Trimester	A twelve-week grading period.

Sample Grade Reports

On the next pages are four sample grade reports for an entire grading period. Each report is set up under a standards-based model. However, all four grade reports have slightly different formats for labeling assignments, scoring assignments, and breaking up assessments into multiple assignments. We encourage you to spend time looking at each report to note these subtle differences and to find the reporting method you think is best for you and your students.

Student: **Ellen Saiers**
Class: **US History Standard**

Average: **79.00%**

Industrial Development 20%		
Assignment	**Points Possible**	**Points Earned**
Test 1: War's impact on industrialization	10	5
Test 1: Disparity among groups	10	7
Test 1: Grant administration	10	6
Test 1: Western migration	10	8
Test 2: Urban growth	10	9
Test 2: Urban vs rural	10	7
Test 2: Impact of western expansion	10	6
Test 3: Civil service reform	10	7
Test 3: Political machines	10	5
Test 3: Populism	10	9
Test 3: Labor unions	10	8
Industry leaders presentation	50	42
	Category Average: **74.38%**	

Emergence of Modern America 30%		
Assignment	**Points Possible**	**Points Earned**
Test 4: American Imperialism	10	8
Test 4: Consequences of Imperialism	10	8
Test 4: Changes in 20's	10	9
Test 4: Prosperity on Eve of Depression	10	7
Test 4: African Americans in Progressive Era	10	8
Test 5: Countries of power WWI	10	6
Test 5: US Involvement in WWI	10	7
Test 5: The Progressive Era	10	8
Test 5: Innovations and Inventions	10	9
Aspects of WWI Pamphlet	40	28
Sum and Difference Identities	6	6
	Category Average: **75.38%**	

The Great Depression and World War II 50%		
Assignment	**Points Possible**	**Points Earned**
Test 6: Impact of Depression on America	10	9
Test 6: Cultural Response to Great Depression	10	9
Test 6: Stock Market Crash	10	8
Test 6: Effects of New Deal	10	8
Test 6: The New Deal	10	9
Test 7: WWII Effects at Home	10	7
Test 7: WWII Begins	10	8
Test 7: Events of WWII	10	8
Test 7: Country Alliances WWII	10	5
WWII Advertisement	20	18
Great Depression Journal	15	14
	Category Average: **82.40%**	

Student: **Steve England**
Class: **English II Honors**

Average: **81.00%**

Language 15%

Assignment	Points Possible	Points Earned
Test Identifying Proper Pronouns	100	100
Test Identifying Adjective and Adverb Phrases	100	79
Test Identifying Verbal Phrases	100	18
Test Appositives	100	100
Test Dangling and Misplaced Modifers	100	90
	Category Average: **77.40%**	

Literature and Informational Text 40%

Assignment	Points Possible	Points Earned
Test Dante's Inferno Literary Devices Symbolism/Allegory	100	94
Test Dante's Inferno Reading Comprehension	100	100
Paper and Poster Dante Informational Text Biography	100	89
Group Presentation Dante's Inferno Historical Context	100	25
Character Sense-o-gram Dante's Inferno Characterization	100	86
	Category Average: **78.80%**	

Writing and research 45%

Assignment	Points Possible	Points Earned
Note-taking and Prewriting Strategies	100	81
Thesis Statement and Outline	100	100
First Draft Research paper	100	100
First revision: Proofreading and Rewriting	100	100
MLA Format & Source Citation	100	44
	Category Average: **85.00%**	

Student: **Ming Wu** Average: **81.00%**
Class: **Chemistry**

Matter and Energy 10%

Assignment	Points Possible	Points Earned
Physical Properties of Matter	10	9
Chemical Properties of Matter	10	10
		Category Average:**95.00%**

Periodic Table and Trends 15%

Assignment	Points Possible	Points Earned
Identification of Elements	10	10
Representative Elements	10	9
Transition Elements	10	9
Inner Transition Elements	10	9
Metal, Non-Metal, Metalloid	10	10
		Category Average: **94.00%**

Mathematics of Chemical Equations 30%

Assignment	Points Possible	Points Earned
Empirical Formula	10	8
Molecular Formula	10	6
Percent Composition	10	5
Mole Ratio	10	6
Stoichiometry	10	5
Percent Yield	10	7
		Category Average: **61.67%**

Chemical and Nuclear Reaction 30%

Assignment	Points Possible	Points Earned
Balancing Equations	10	5
Synthesis	10	9
Decomposition	10	8
Combustion	10	8
Single Replacement	10	10
Double Replacement	10	9
		Category Average: **81.67%**

Chemical Bonding 15%

Assignment	Points Possible	Points Earned
Compounds	10	10
Covalent Compounds	10	9
Molecular Structure	10	10
		Category Average: **96.67%**

Student: **Tommy Jenkins**
Class: **Pre-Calculus Honors**

Average: **78.00%**

Functions and Graphs 15%

Assignment	Points Possible	Points Earned
Functions and 1-to-1	12	12
Inverse	14	11
Domain and Range	11	2
Transformations	14	14
Asymptotes	9	8
		Category Average:**78.33%**

Trigonometric Functions 40%

Assignment	Points Possible	Points Earned
Angles	16	10
Arc Length	5	9
Solving Right Triangles	18	9
Graphing Trig Functions	16	9
Solving Trig Equations	14	10
		Category Average: **75.36%**

Analytical Trigonometry 45%

Assignment	Points Possible	Points Earned
Empirical Formula	10	8
Molecular Formula	10	6
Percent Composition	10	5
Mole Ratio	10	6
Stoichiometry	10	5
Percent Yield	10	7
		Category Average: **61.67%**

Analytical Trigonometry 45%

Assignment	Points Possible	Points Earned
Verifying Trig Identities	18	8
Sum and Difference Identities	6	6
Law of Sines	12	12
Law of Cosines	12	12
Applications of Laws of Sines and Cosines	16	13
		Category Average: **79.69%**

LaVergne, TN USA
27 February 2011
218094LV00003B/2/P

9 781936 541072